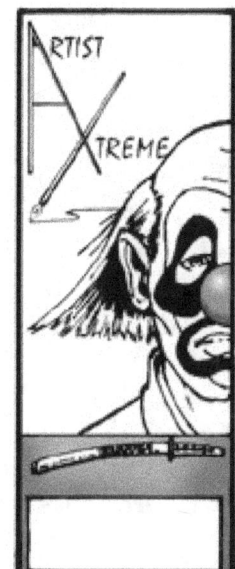

ACTION

ACTION

ACTION

Dedicated to all those that strive to become the next great Comic Book Artist

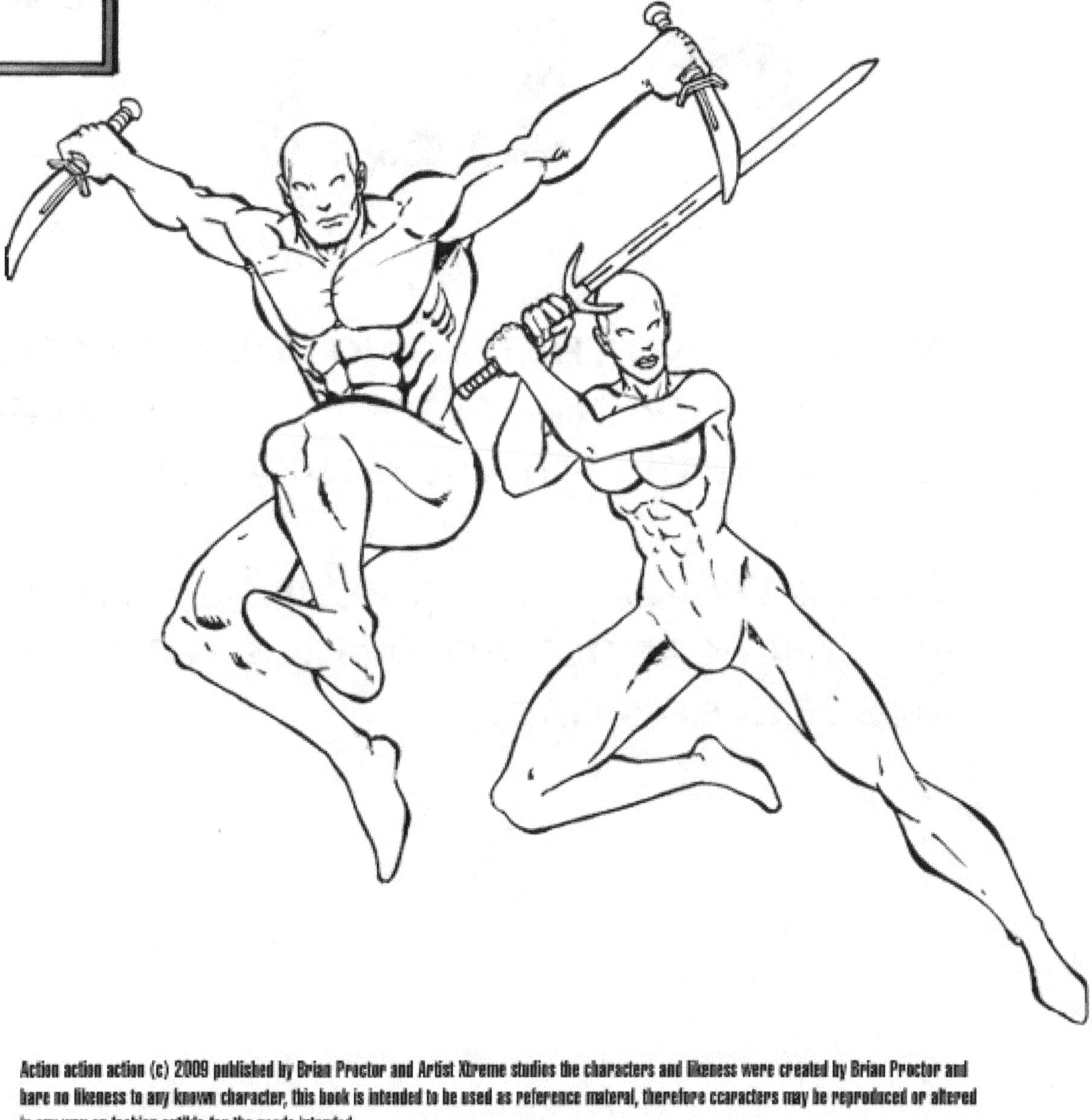

CHAPTER ONE

FLY

WHEN FLYING THERE'S NOT REALLY TOO
MANY DIFFERENT POSITIONS YOU CAN USE,
THE SECRET IS THE CAMERA ANGLE.

TAKE A LOOK AT THESE FLYING POSITIONS
AND THINK ABOUT ADJUSTING THE CAMERA
ANGLE EVEN MORE.

Fly

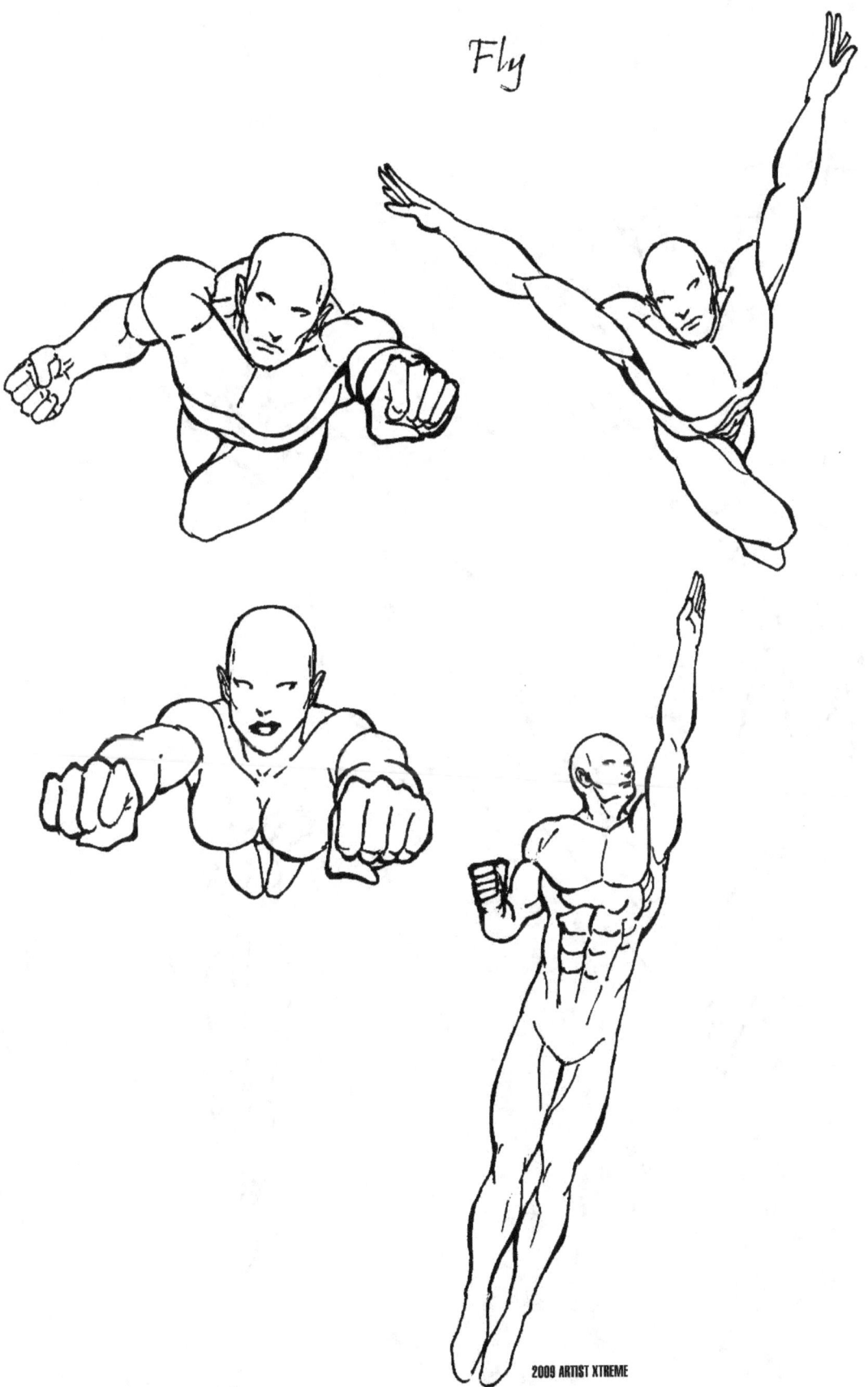

Fly

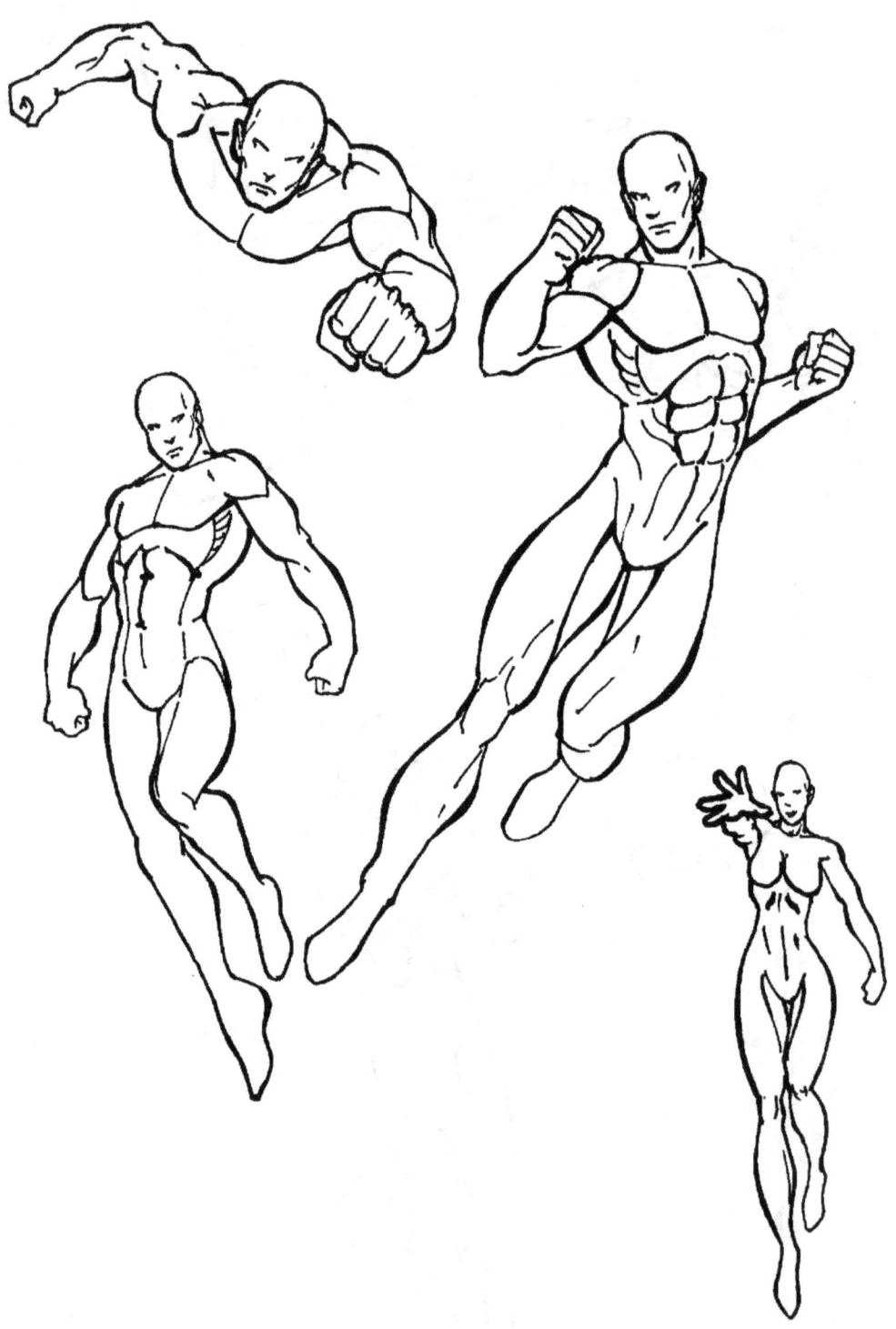

Fly

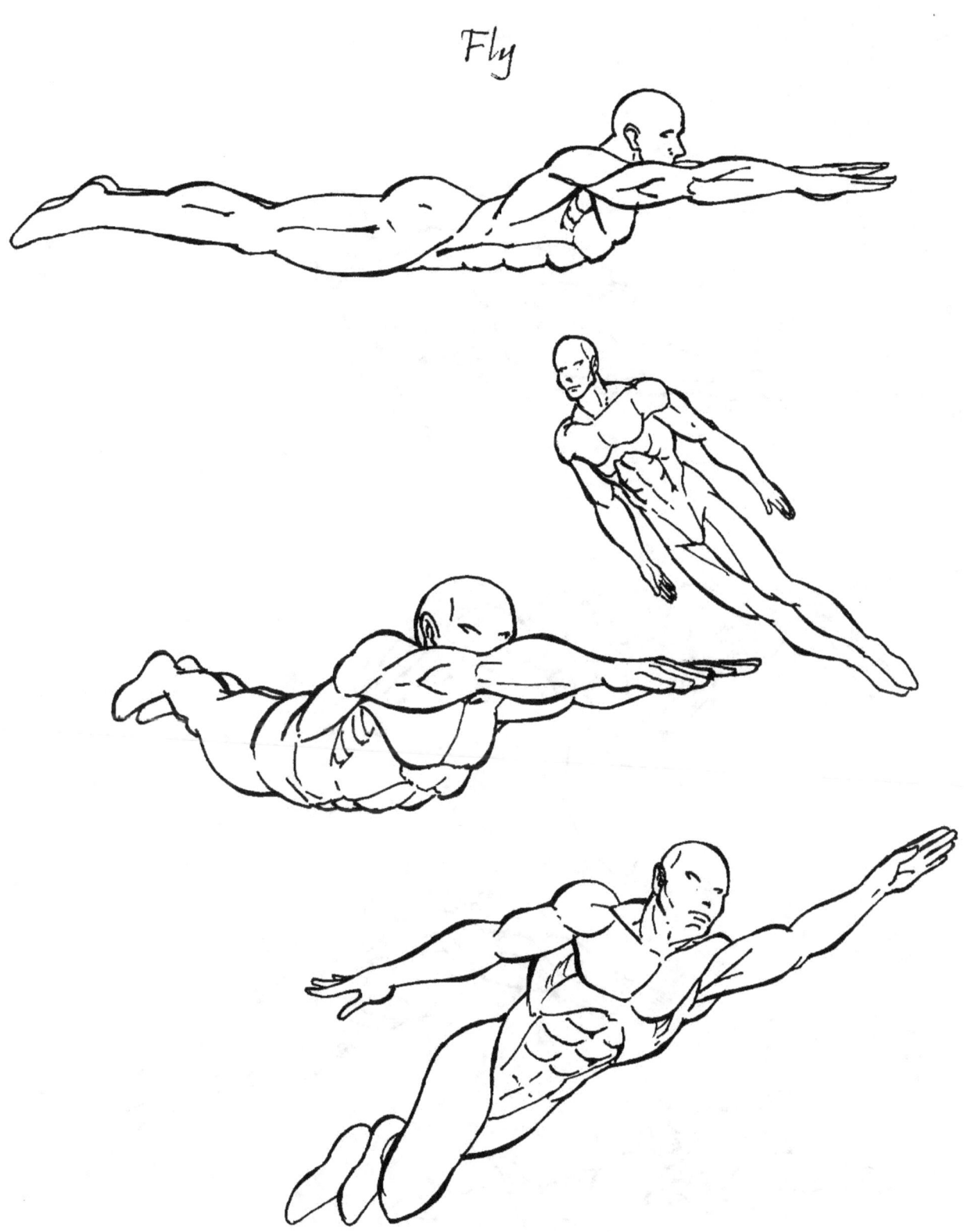

Fly

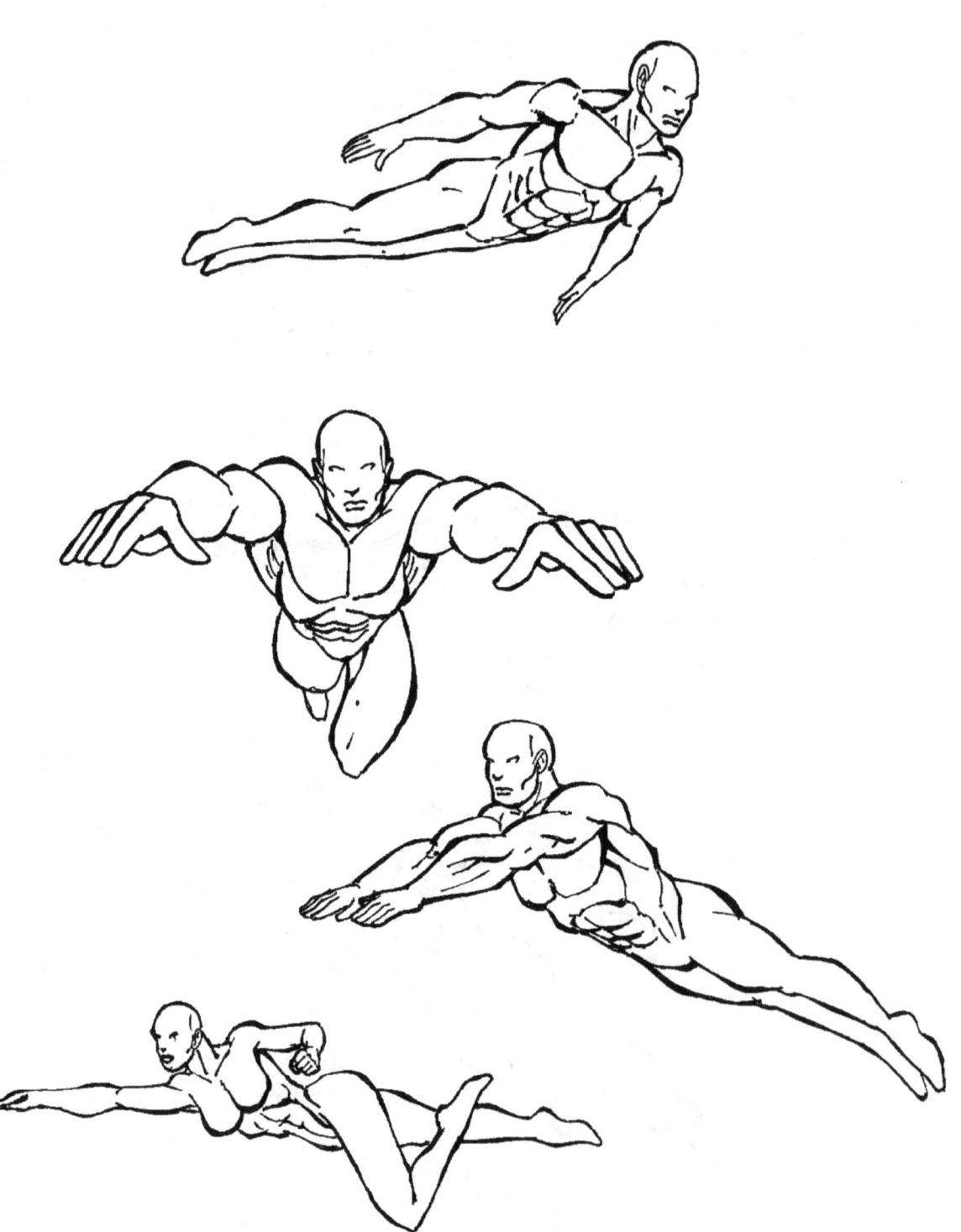

Fly

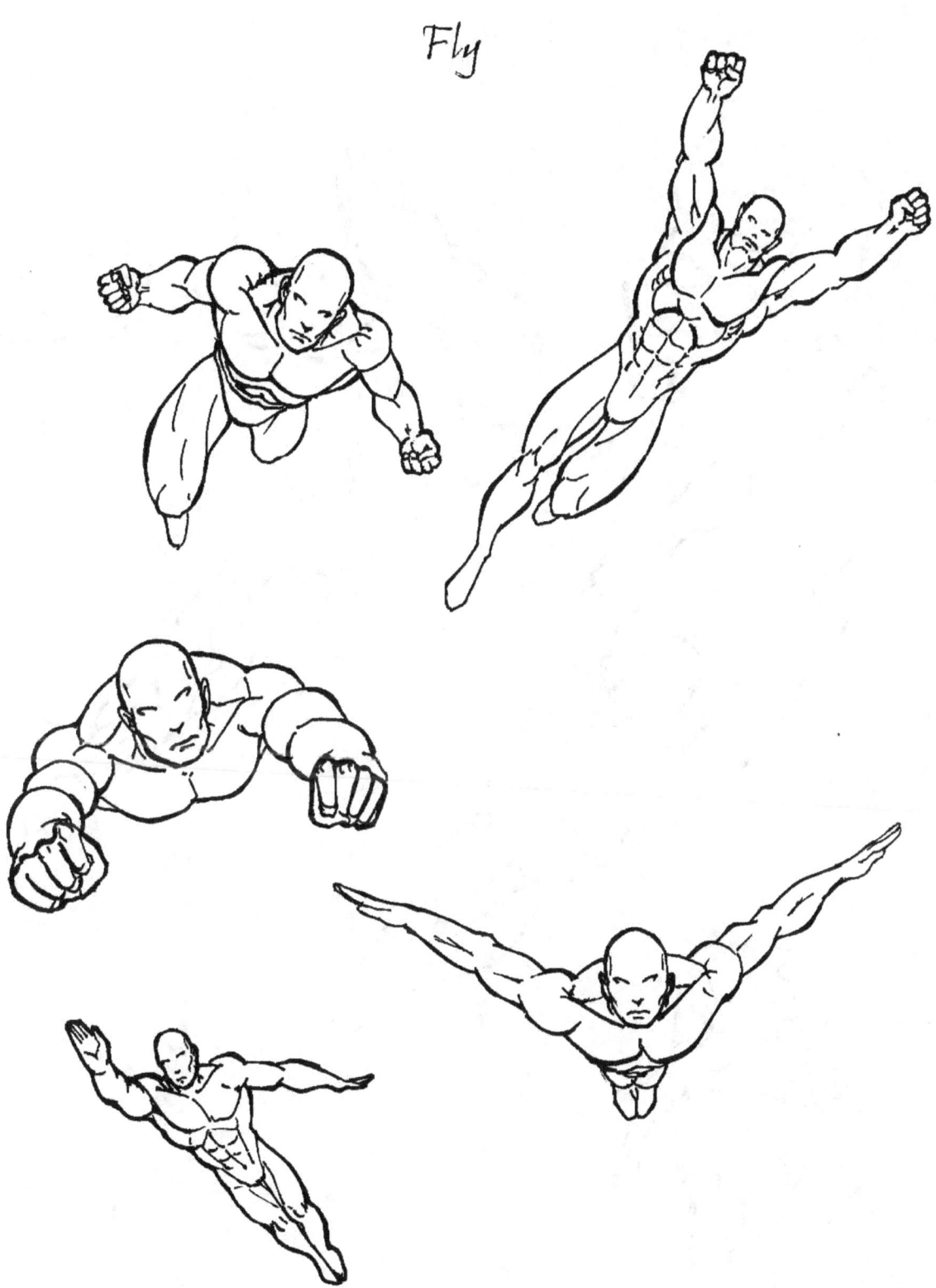

Fly

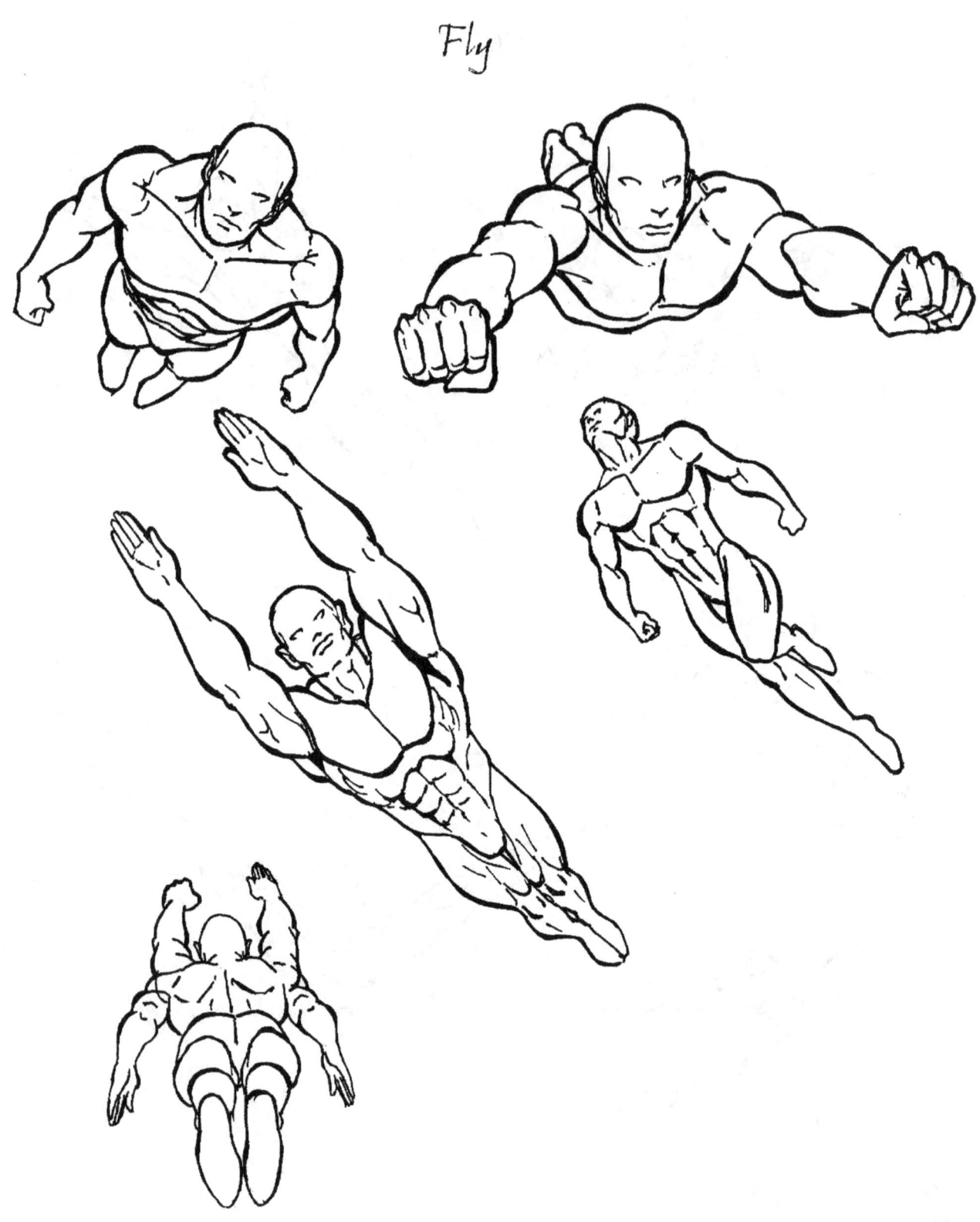

CHAPTER THREE

JUMP

WHENEVER THERE IS A FOOT CHASE,
SOMEONE IS BOUND TO JUMP OVER
SOMETHING, OR LEAP OVER IT OR JUMP
OFF OF IT, OR MAYBE JUST FALL OFF OF IT.

Jump

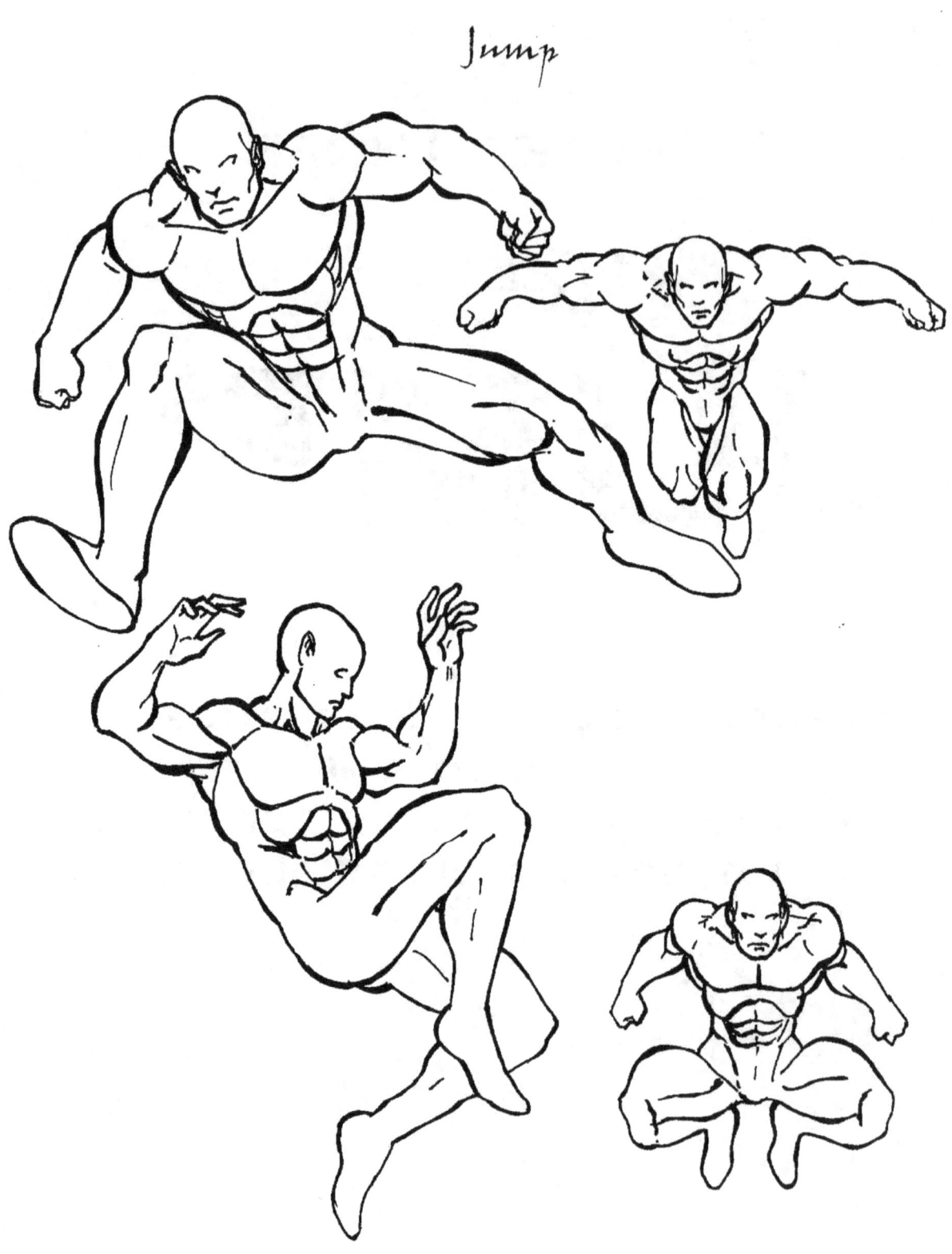

Jump

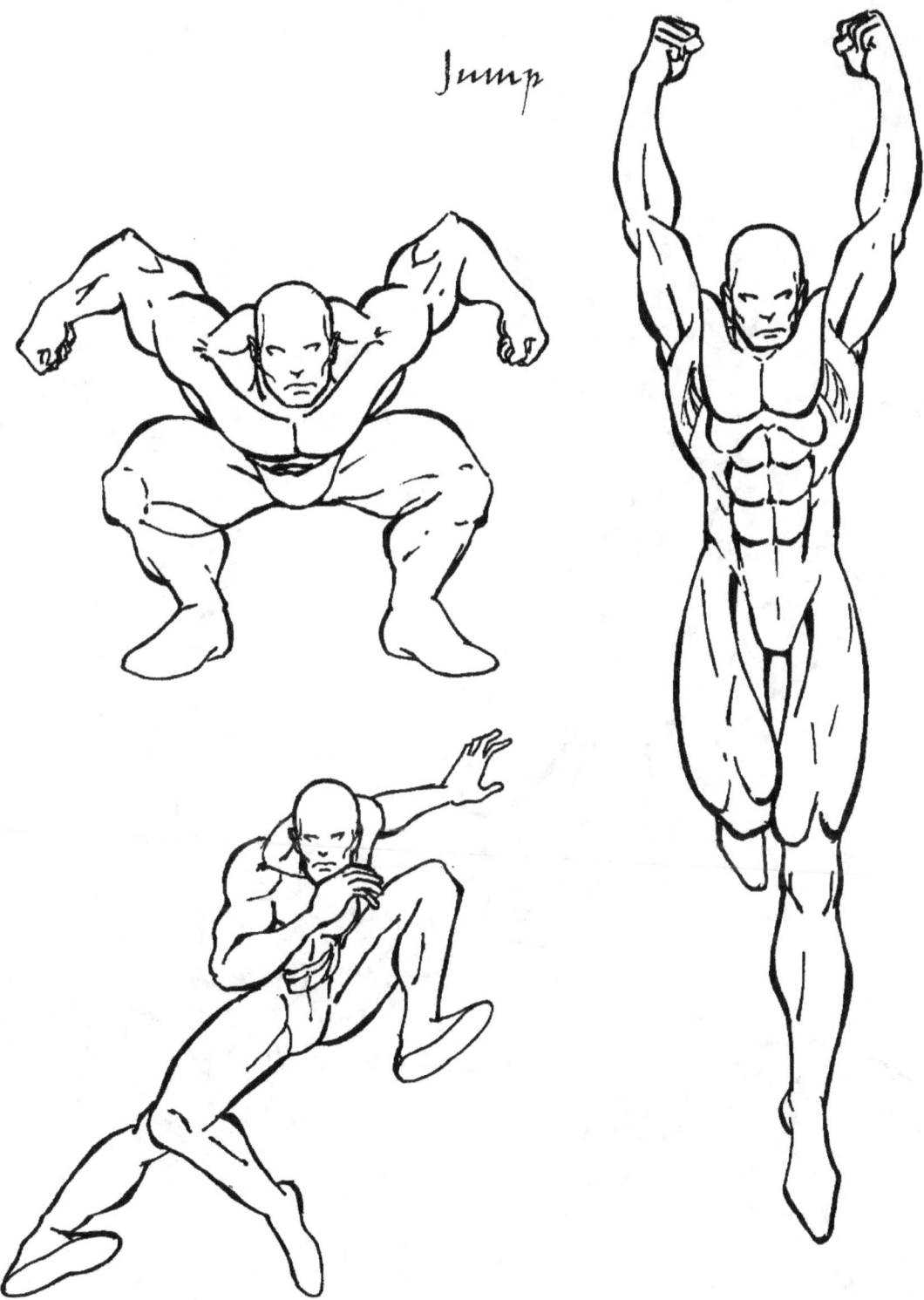

Jump

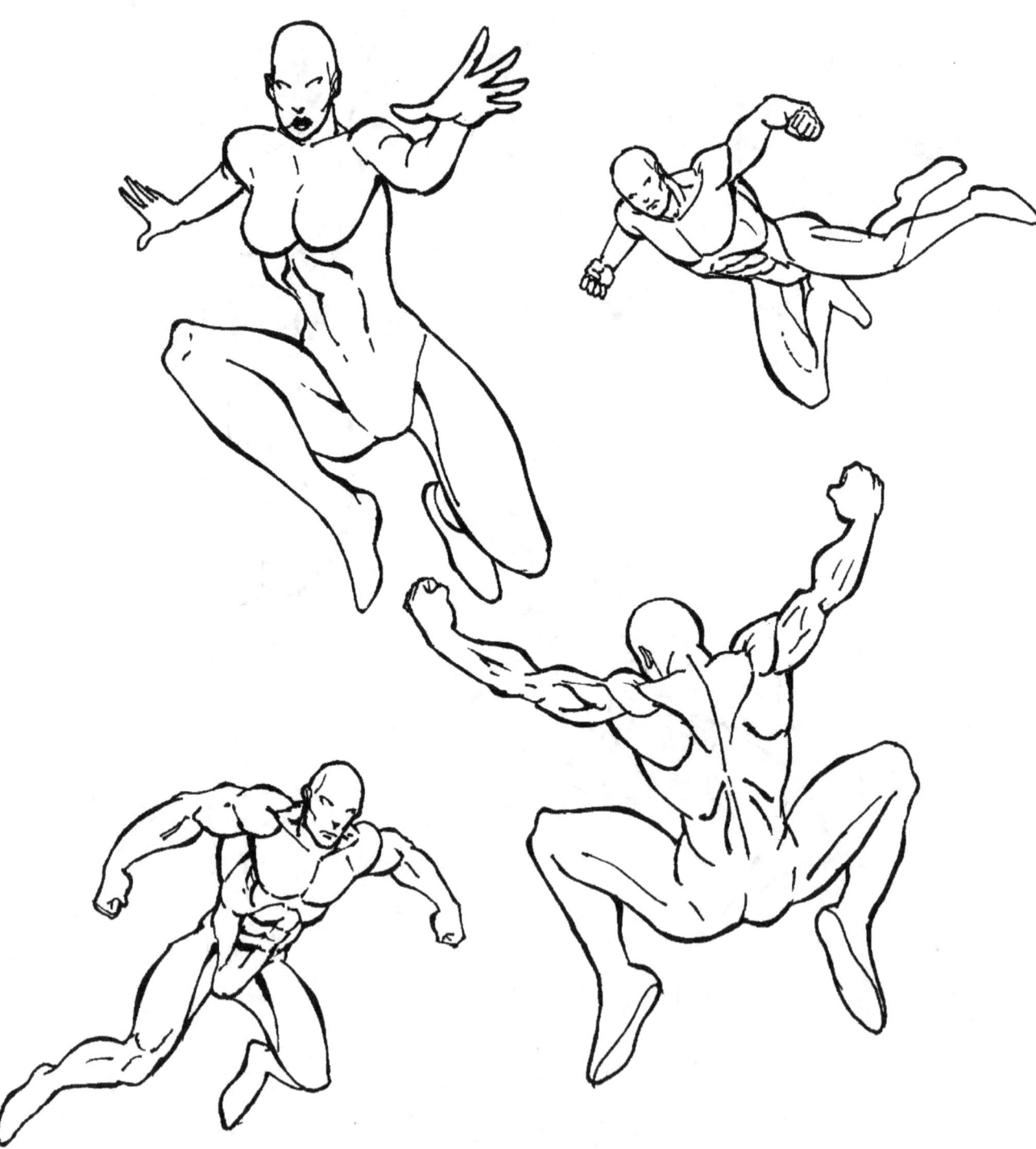

Jump

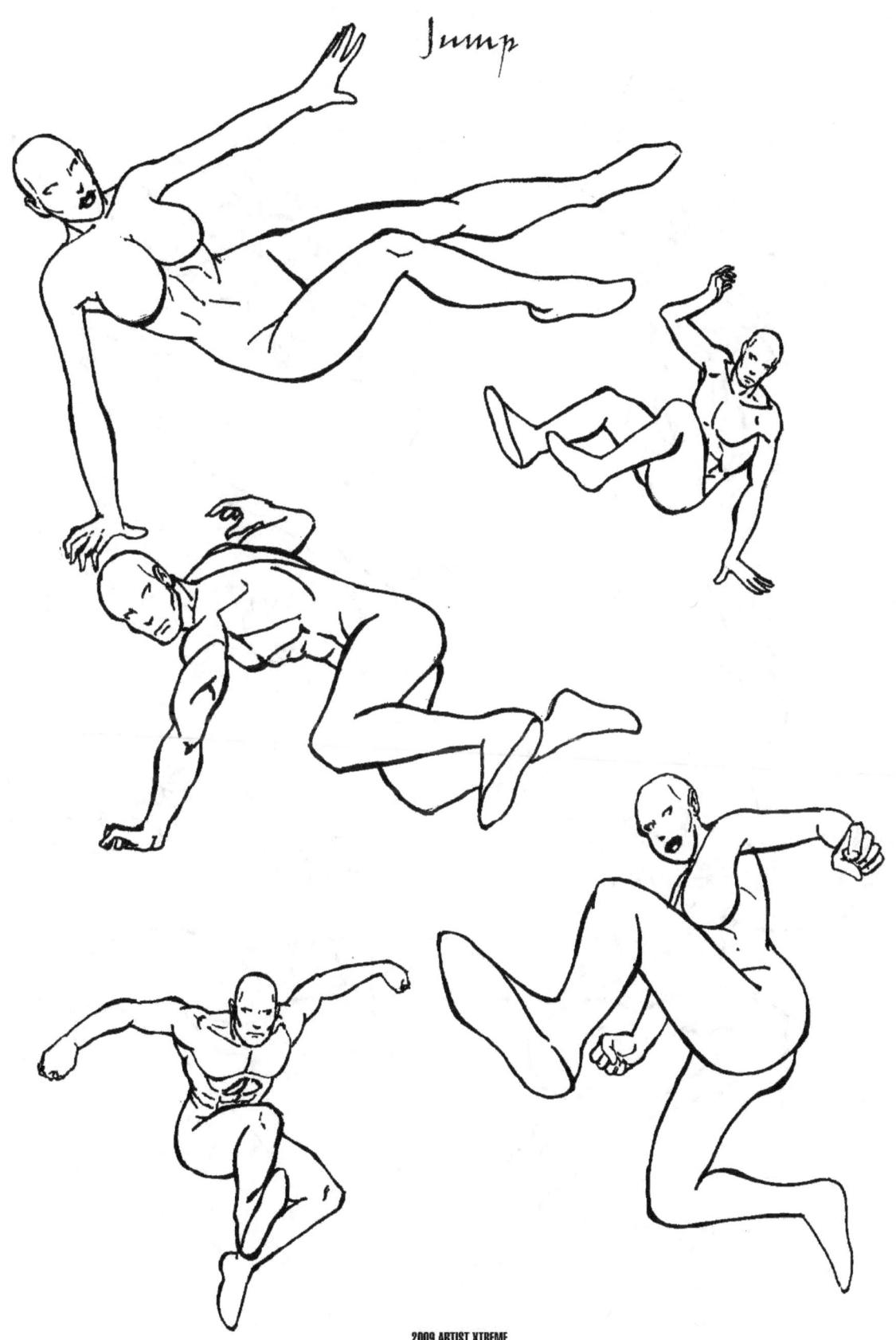

Jump

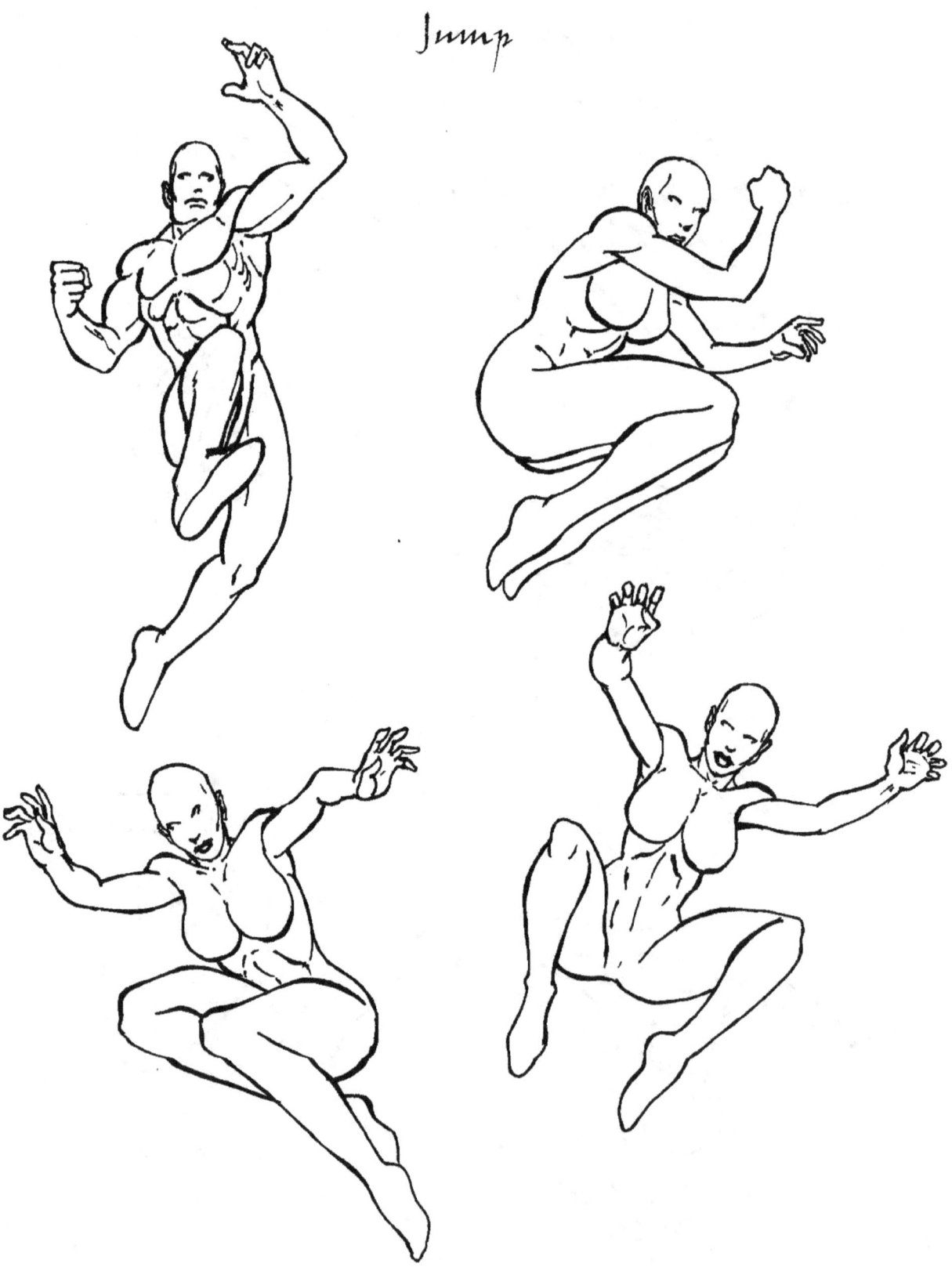

CHAPTER FOUR

KICK

In this chapter we take a look a few different kicks. Nothing gets your attention quicker then a good side kick to the head.

Kick

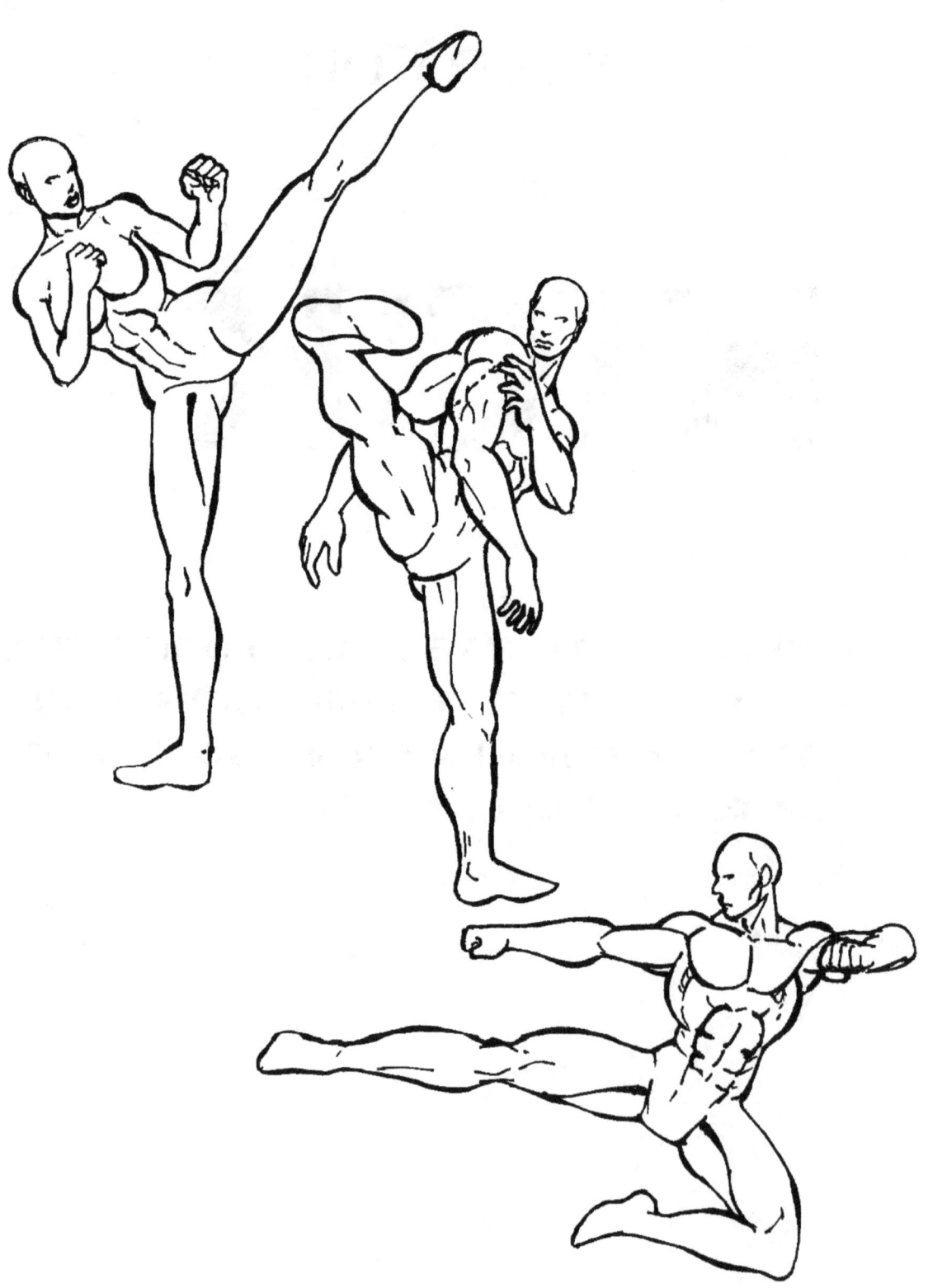

Kick

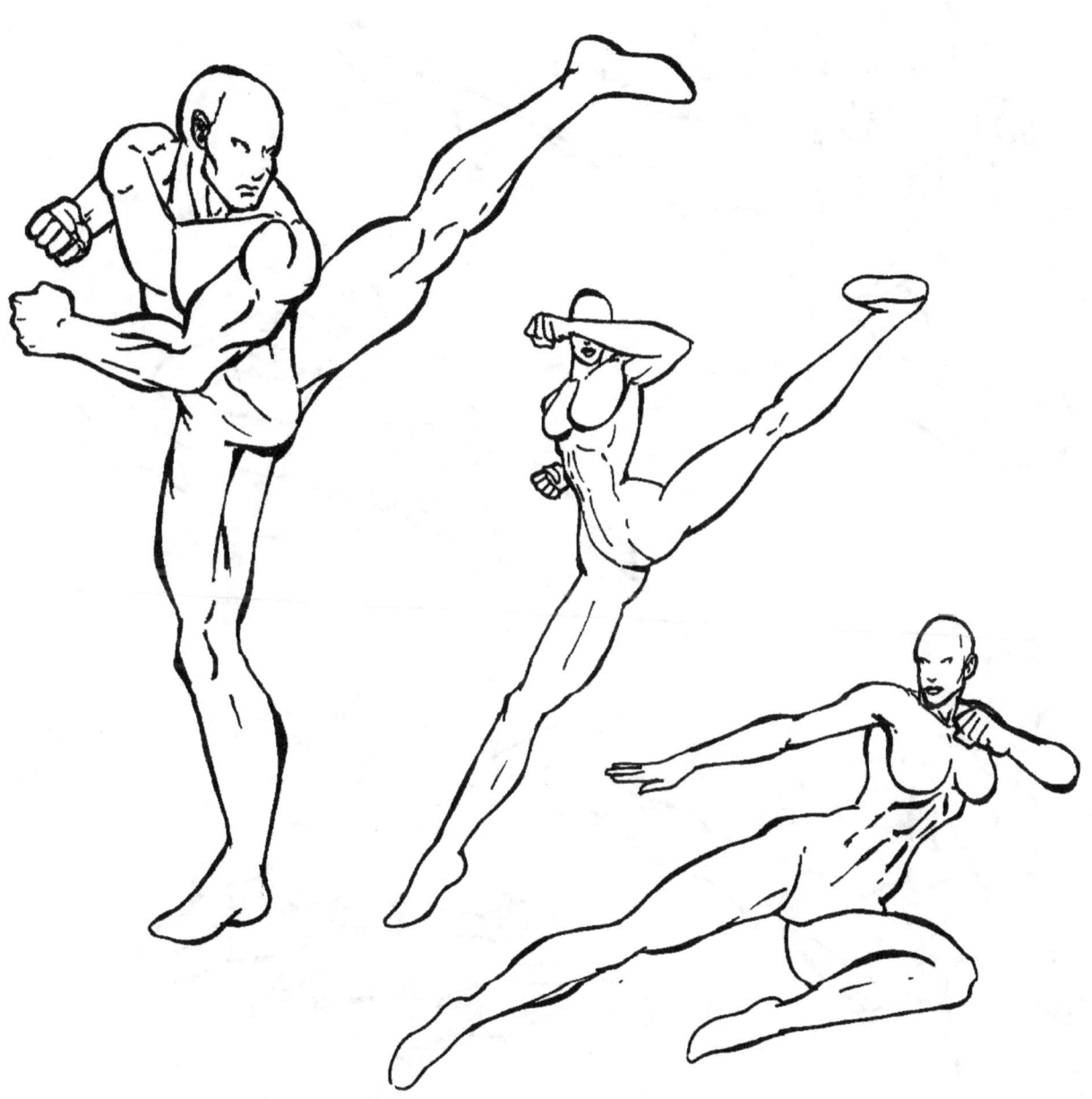

Kick

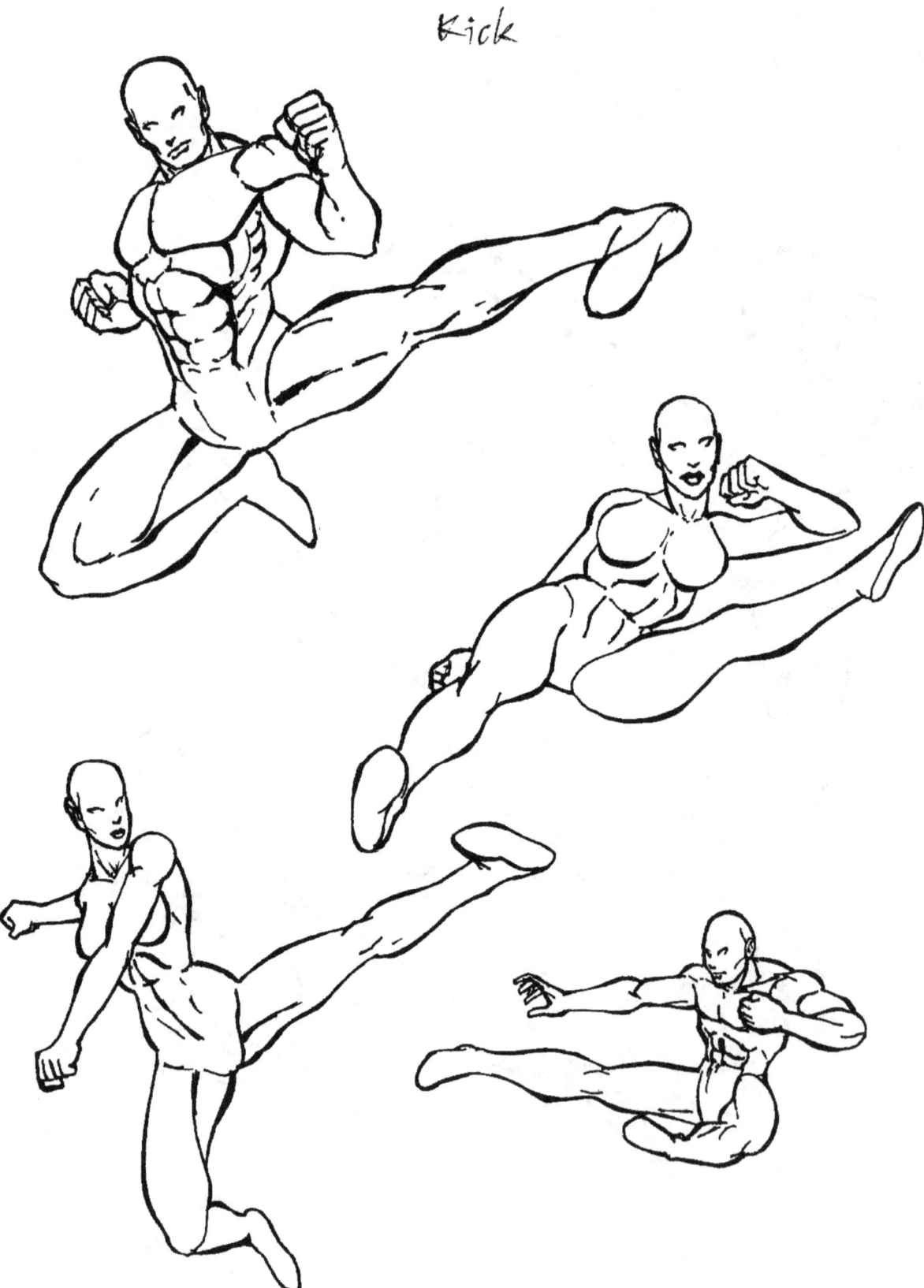

Kick

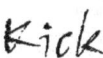

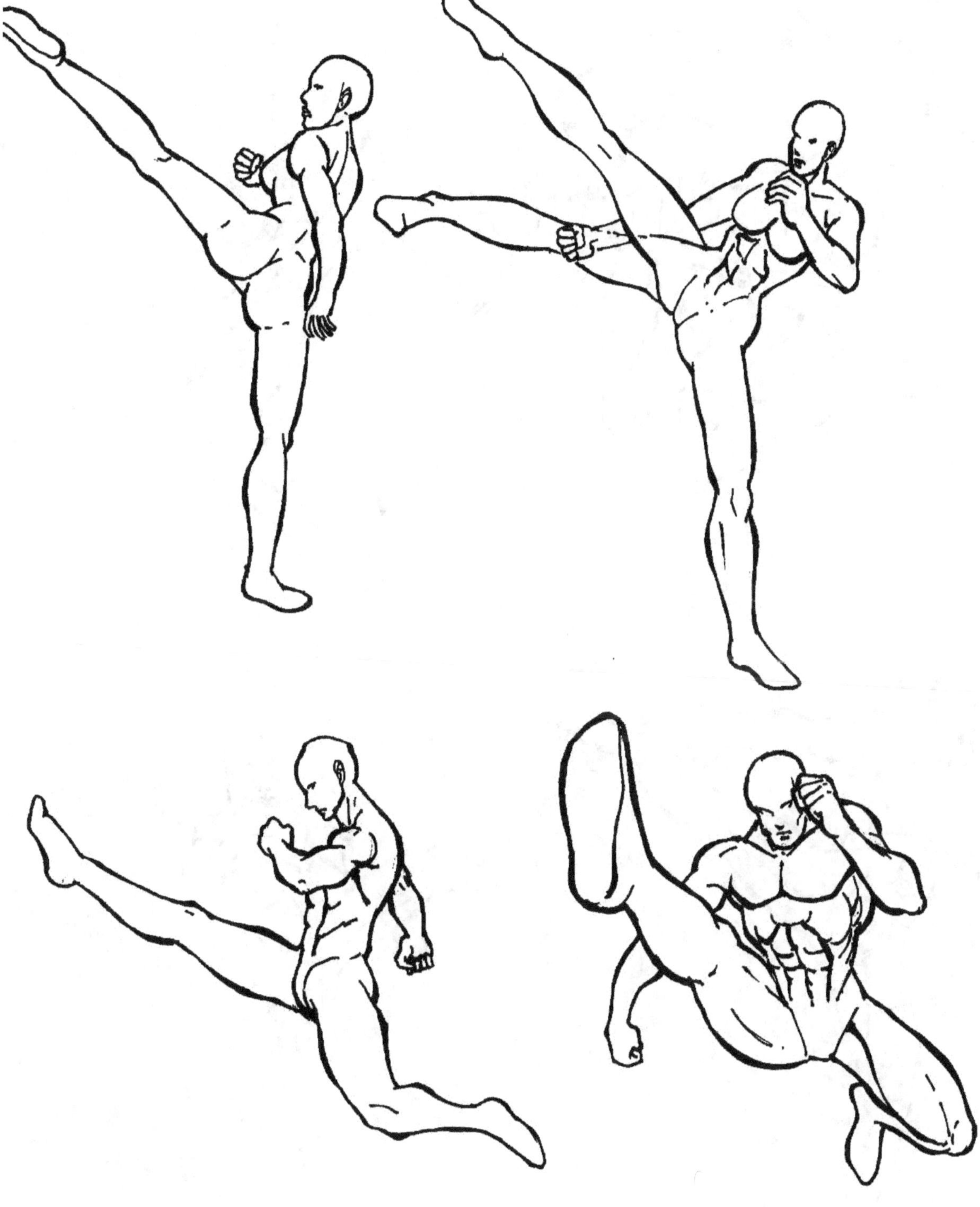

kick

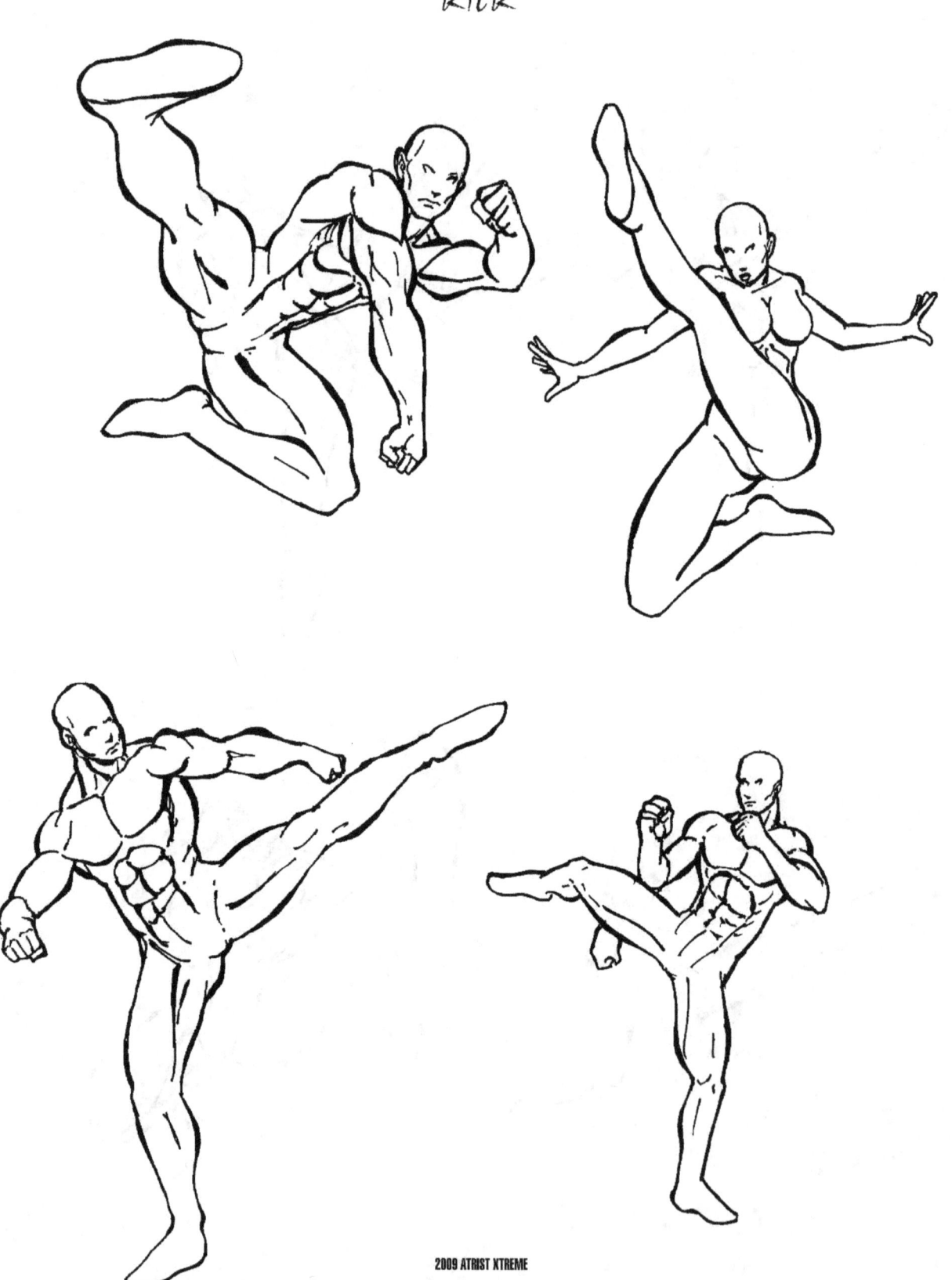

CHAPTER FIVE

PUNCH

LET'S TAKE A LOOK AT SOME VARIOUS PUNCHES AND ANGLES IN WHICH THEY ARE DELIVERED.
REMEMBER, IT'S NOT A GOOD FIGHT IF YOU DON'T HAVE THAT ONE GOOD KNOCK OUT PUNCH.

Punch

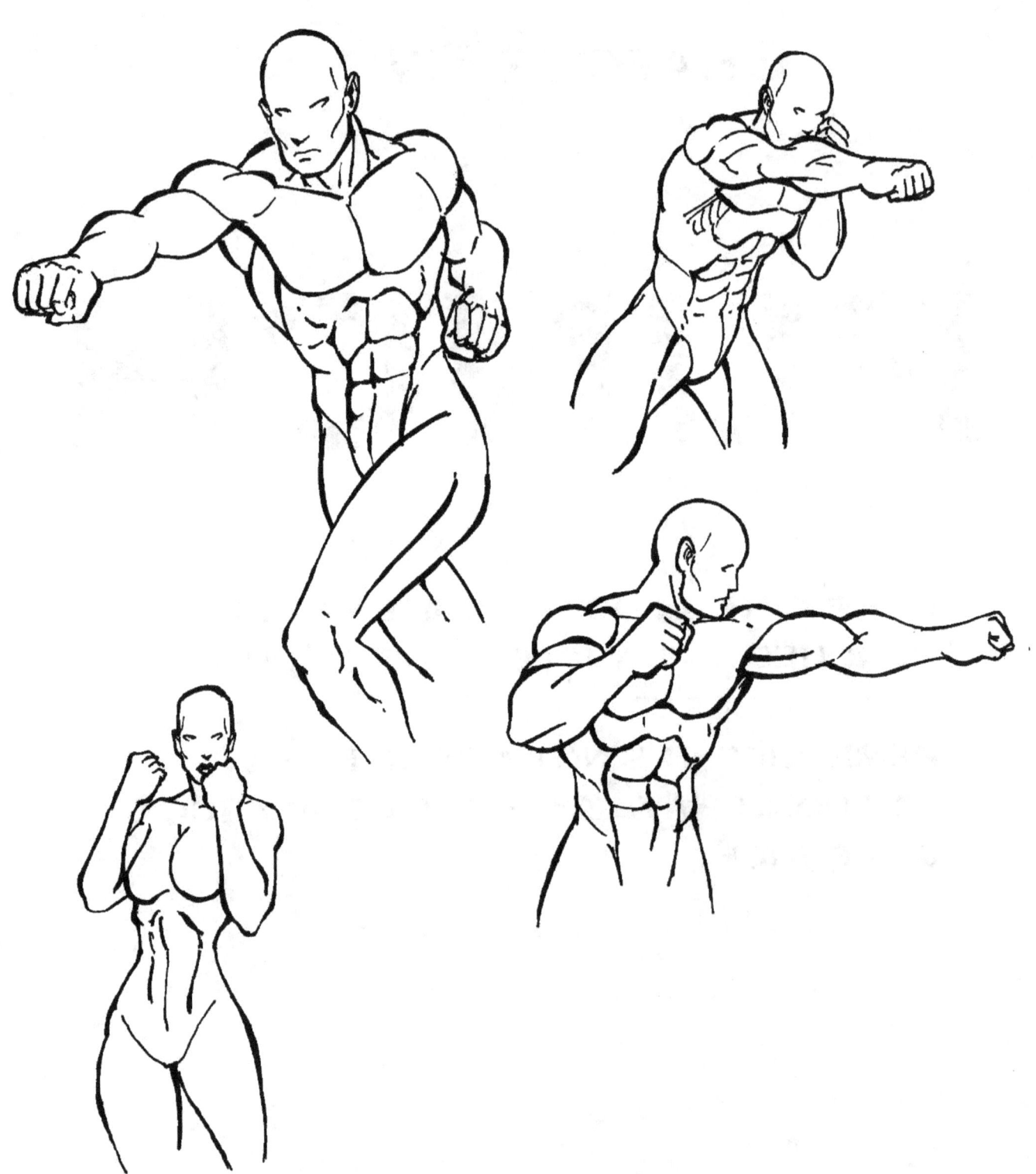

Punch

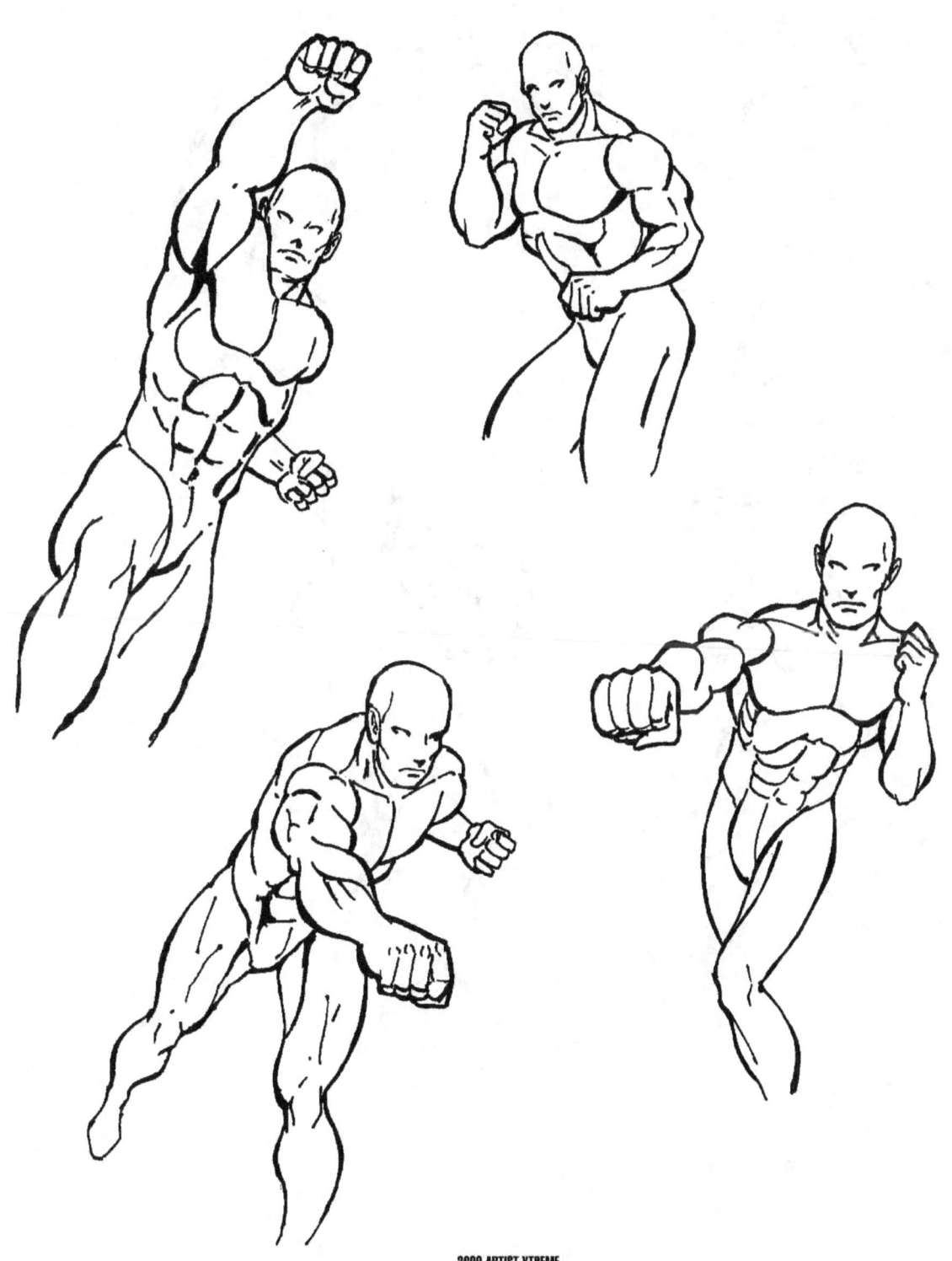

Punch

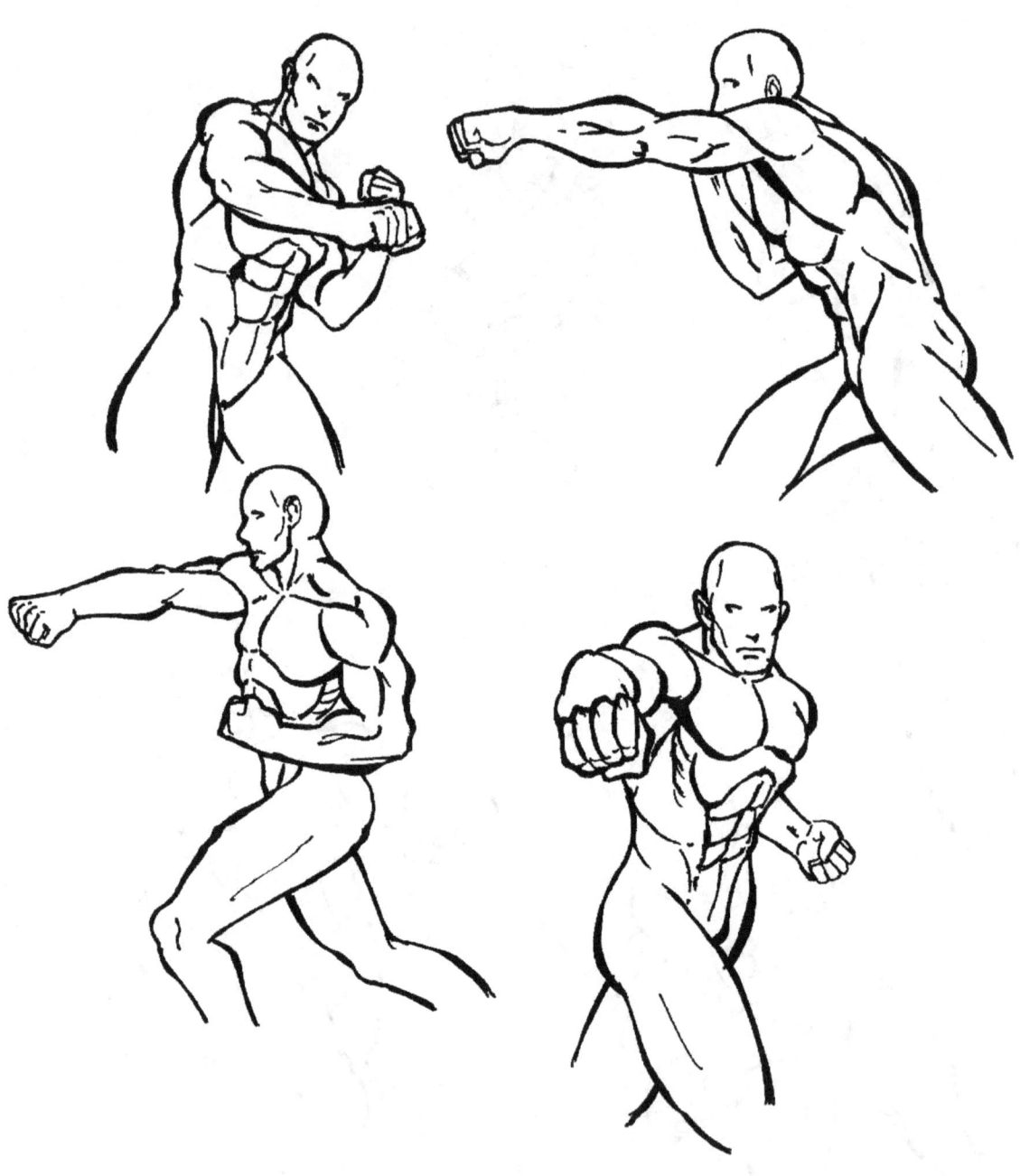

Punch

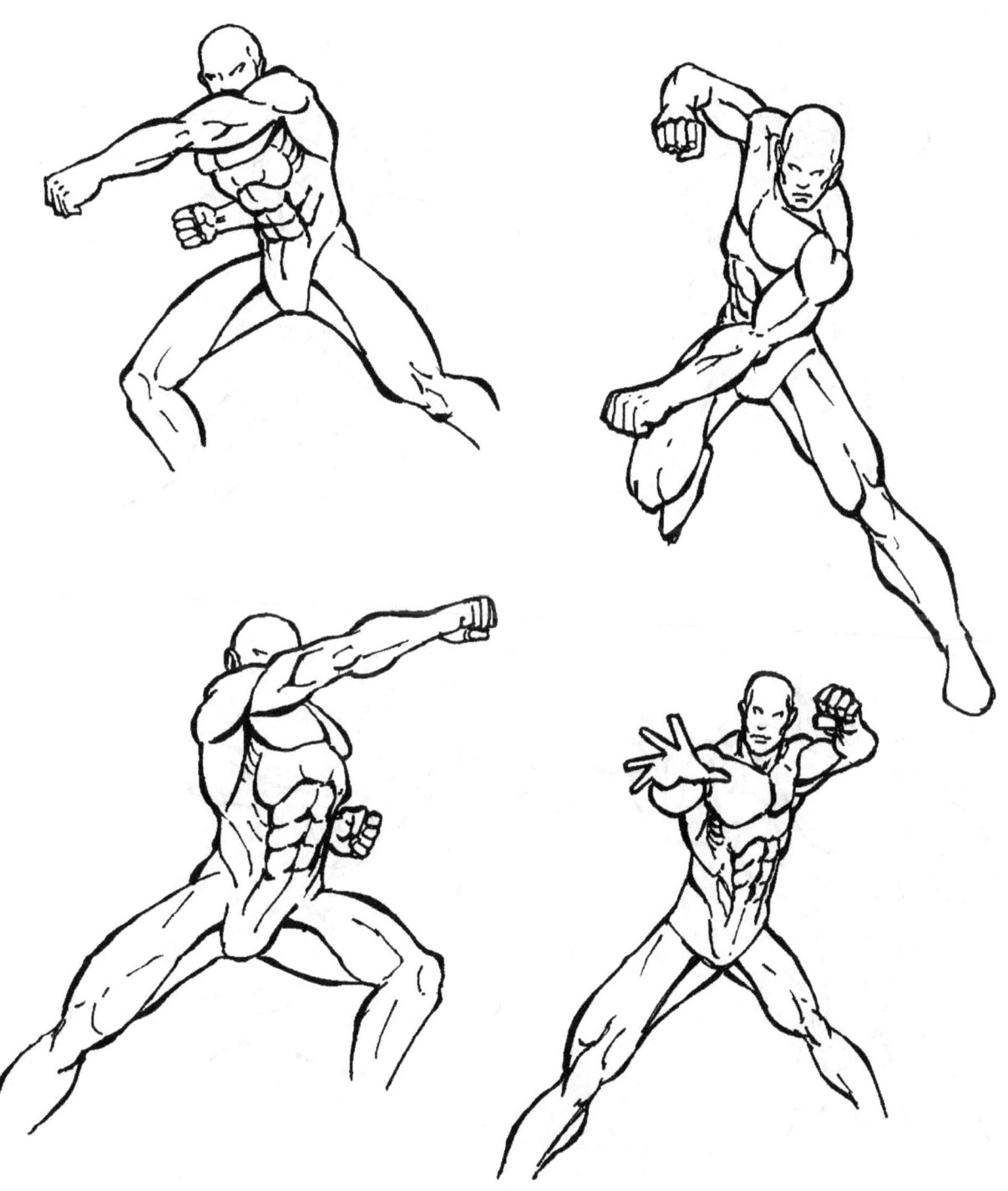

Punch

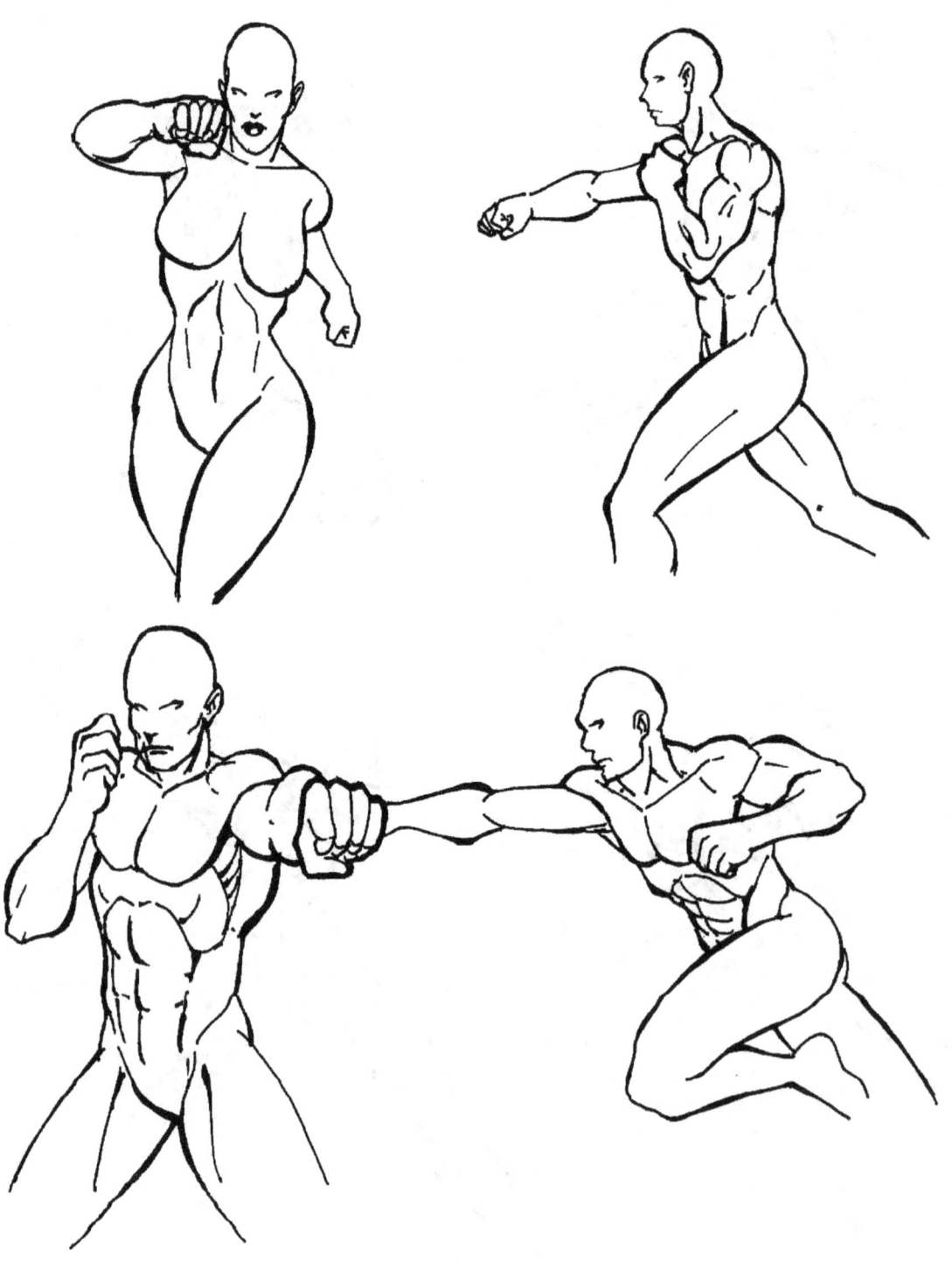

CHAPTER TWO

RUN

WHAT'S A GOOD CHASE IF THERE'S NO RUNNING. EACH RUN IS DIFFERENT DEPENDING ON THE SITUATION WHETHER YOUR CHASING, FLEEING OR JUST GOING FOR A JOG IN THE PARK.

Run

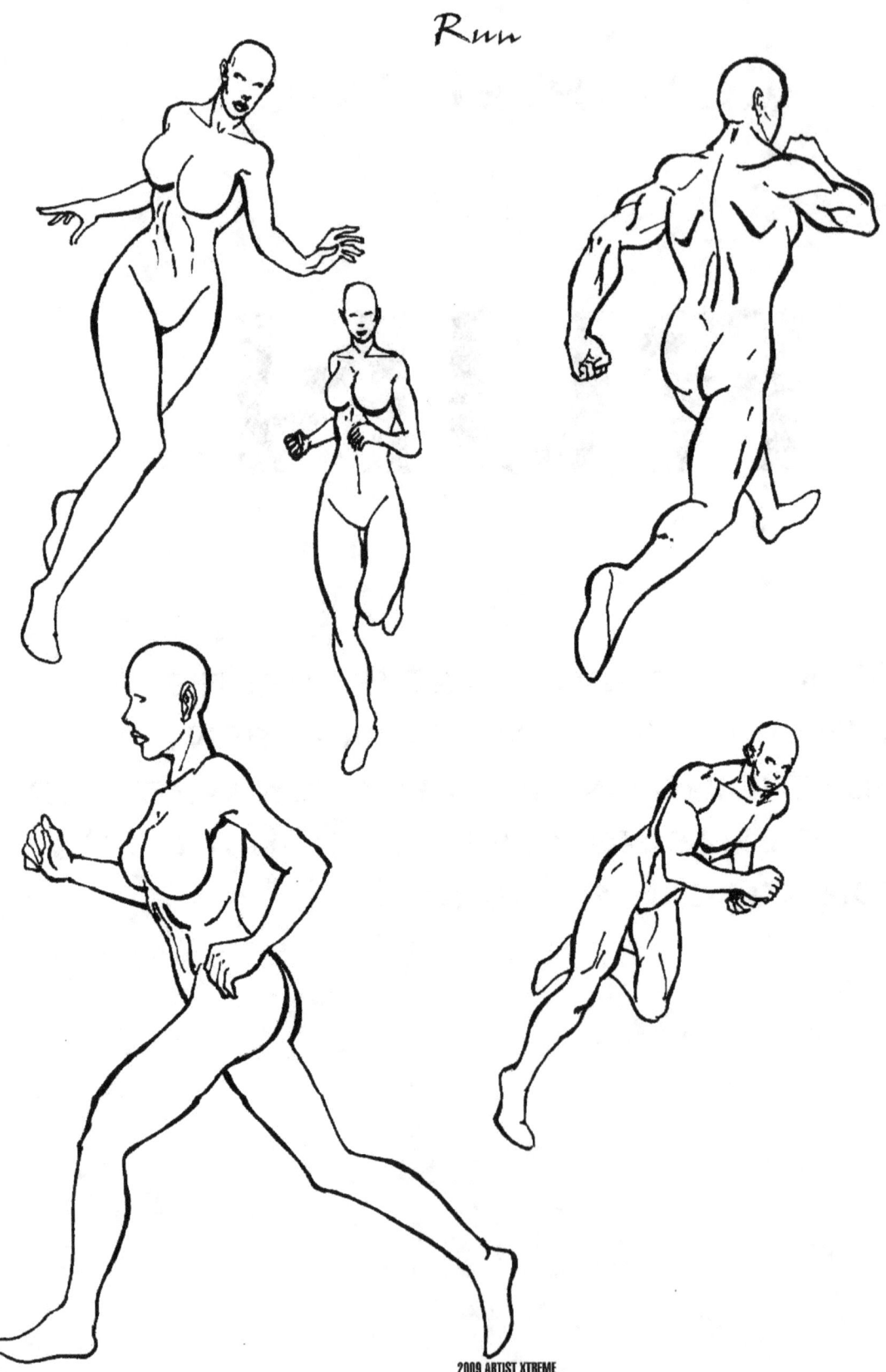

Run

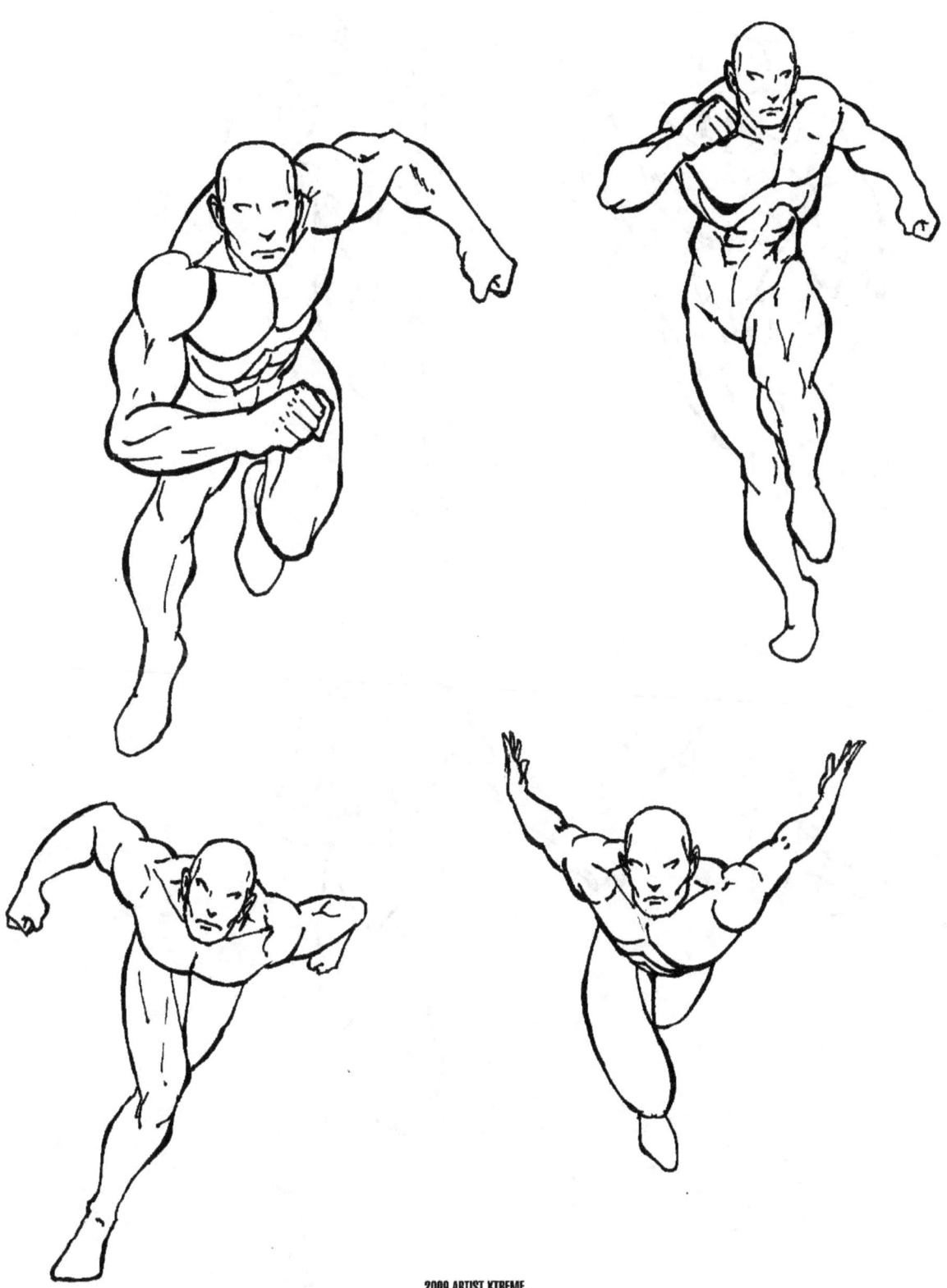

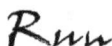

Run

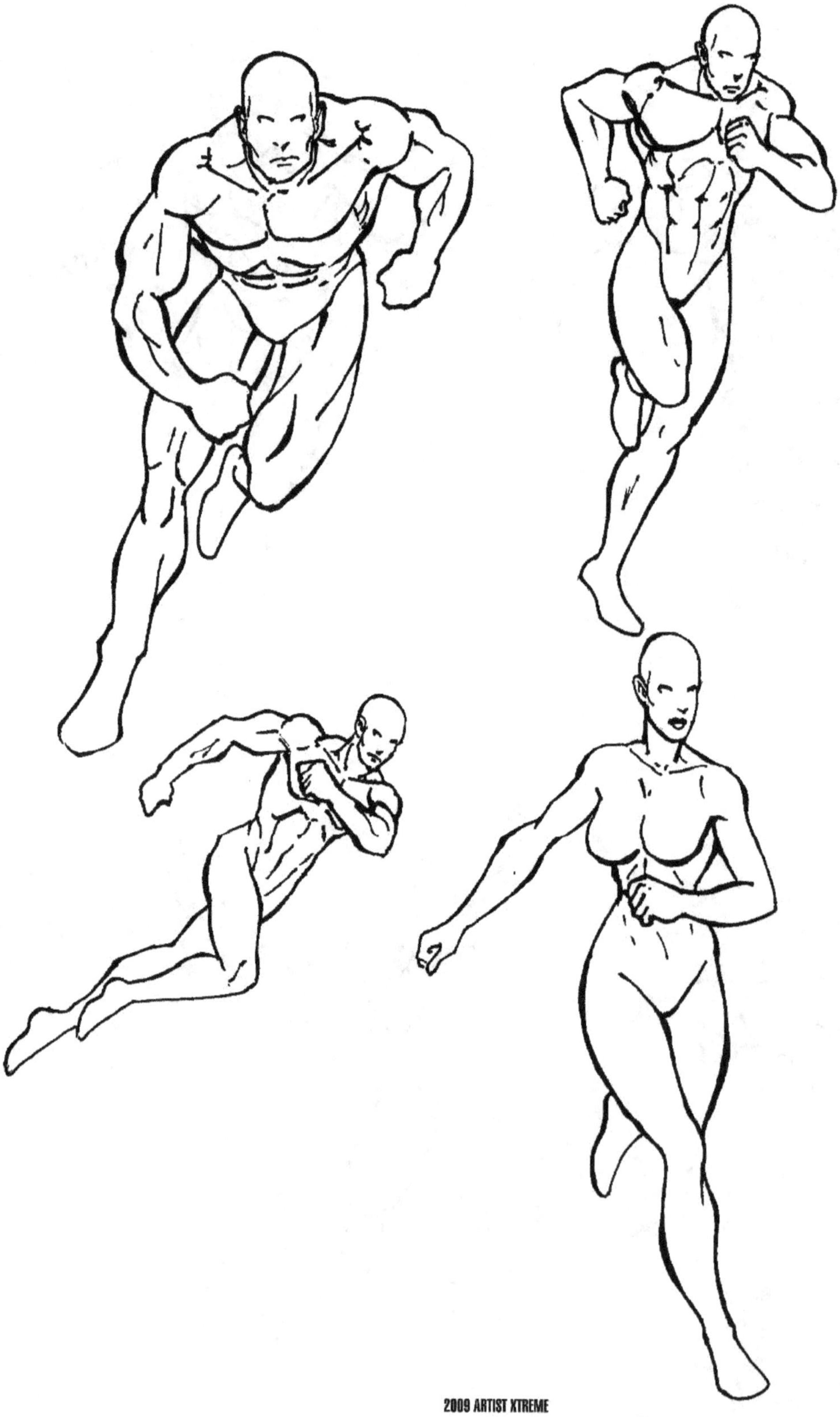

Run

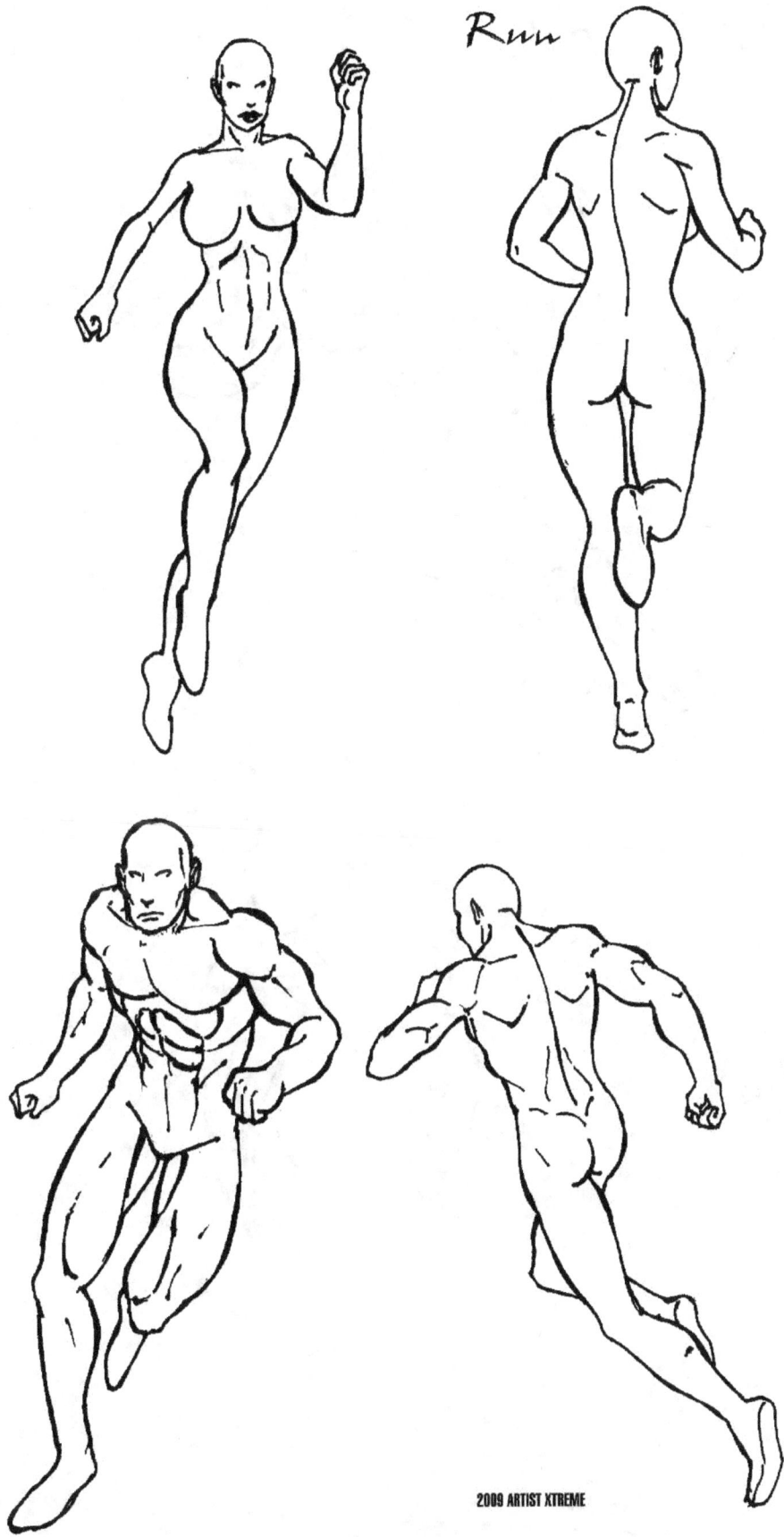

Run

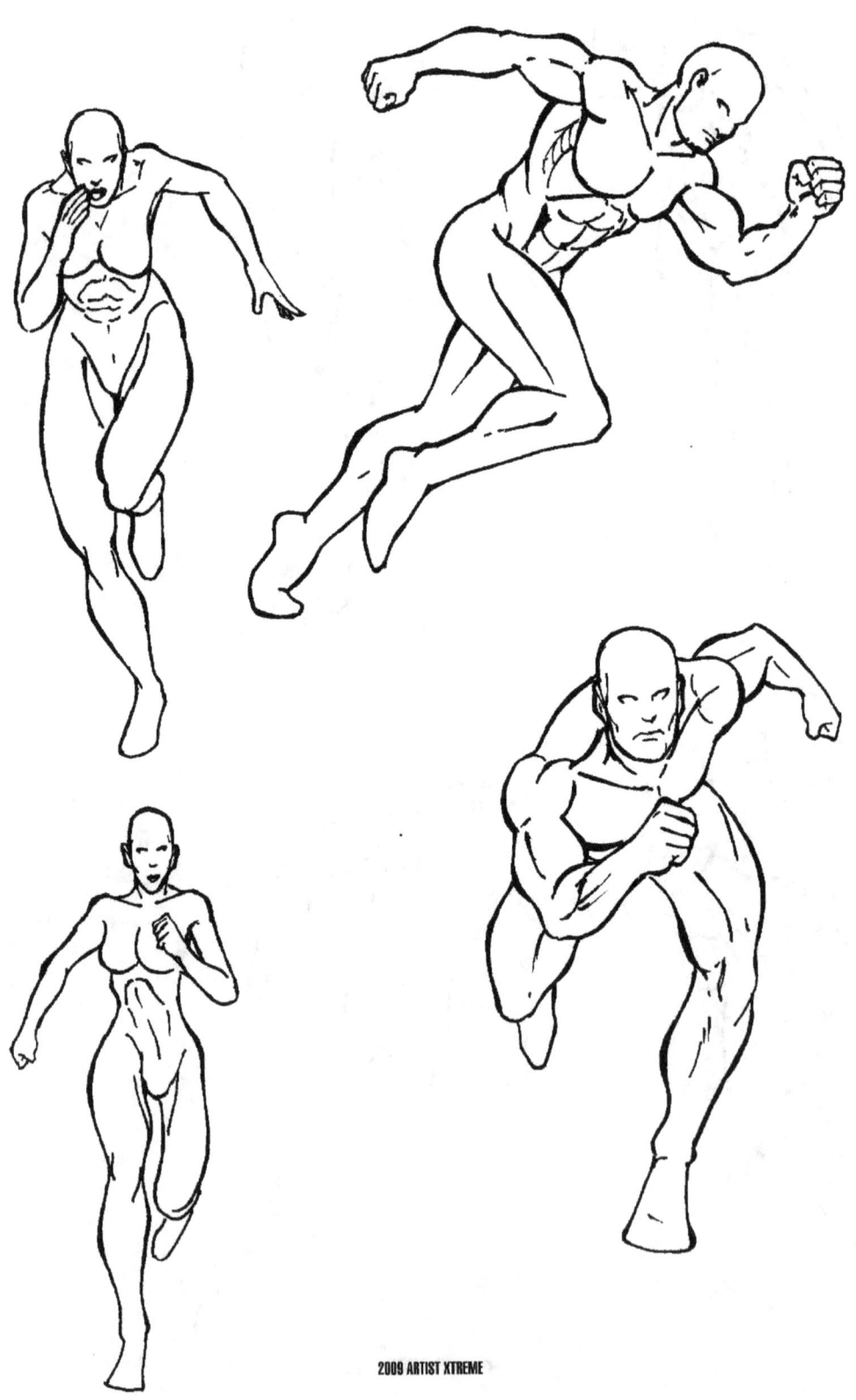

CHAPTER SEVEN

STRIKE A POSE

EVERY GOOD HERO WORTH HIS SALT
KNOWS HOW TO STRIKE A POSE.
IT HAPPENS RIGHT WHEN HE/SHE
ARRIVES ON THE SCENE, JUST BEFORE
THE BATTLE BEGINS OR RIGHT AFTER
THE BATTLE ENDS.

Strike a Pose

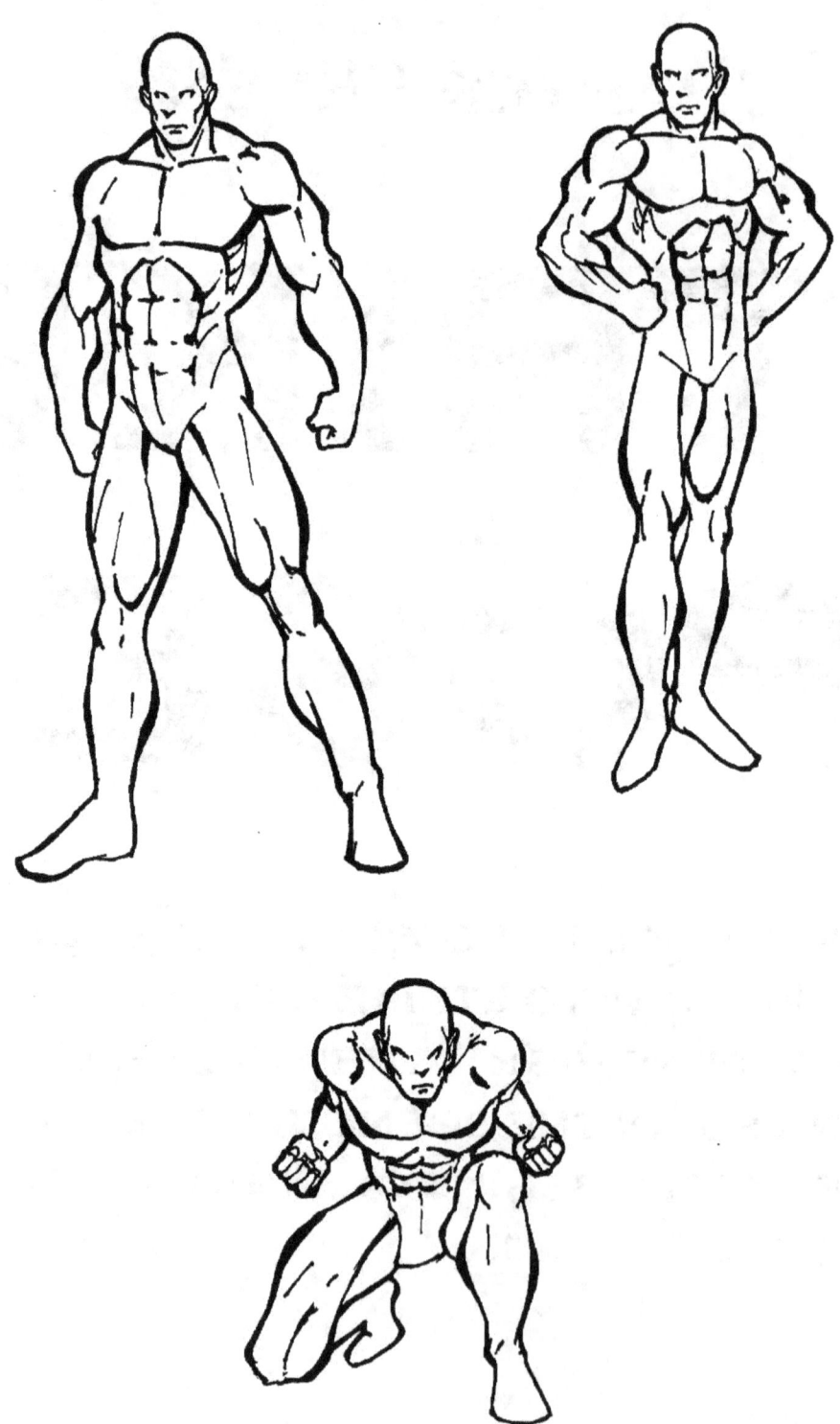

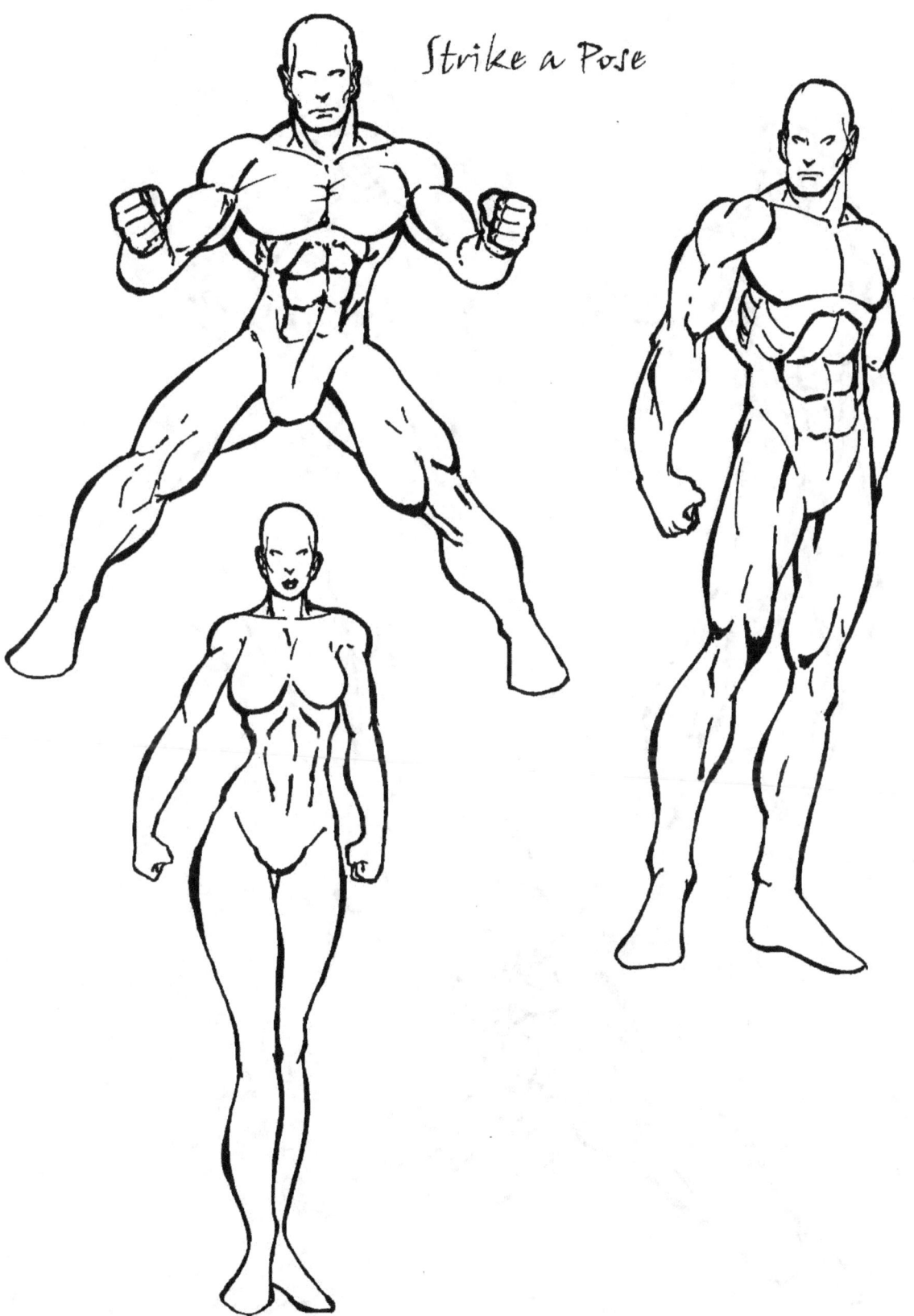

Strike a Pose

Strike a Pose

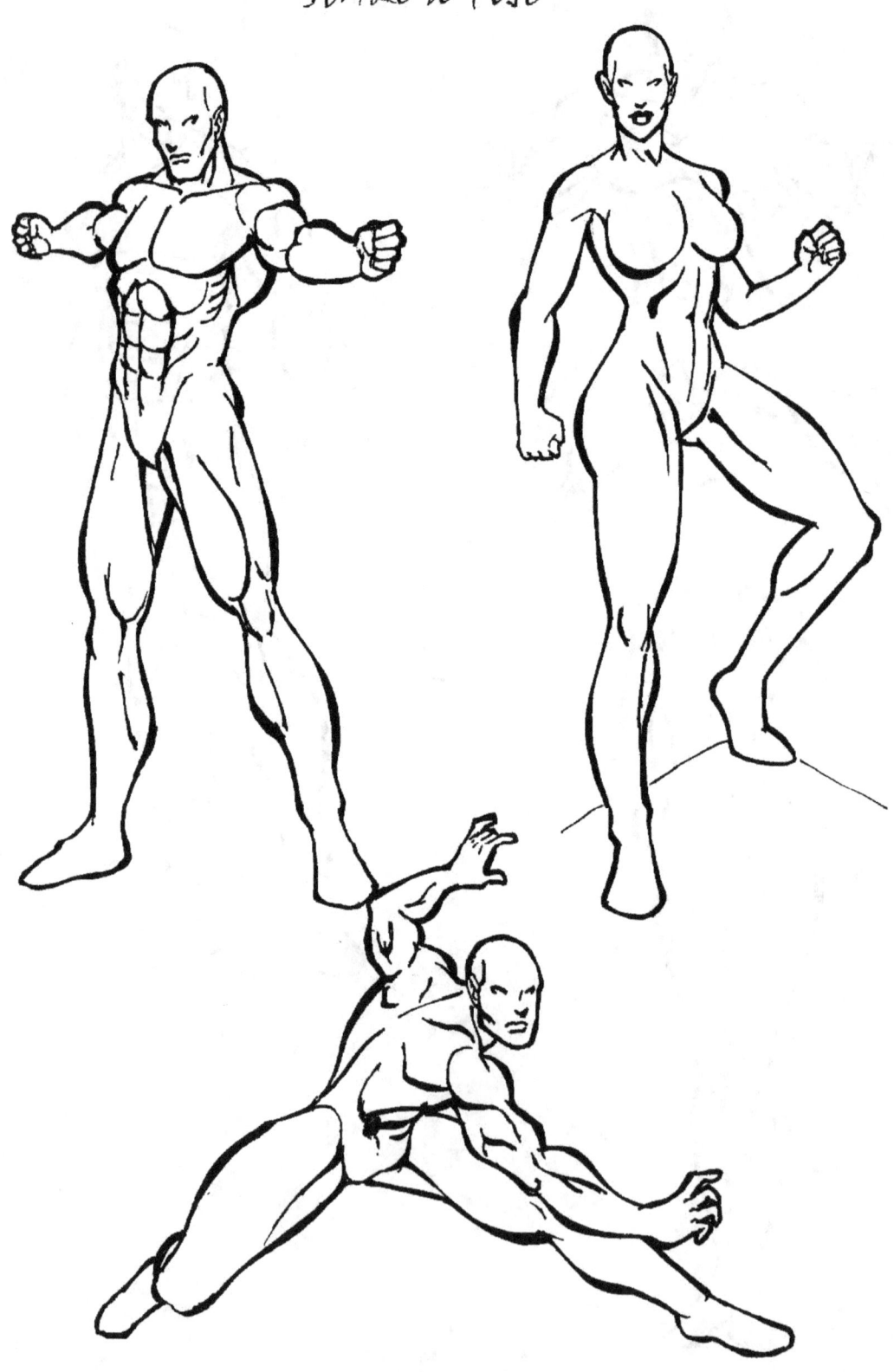

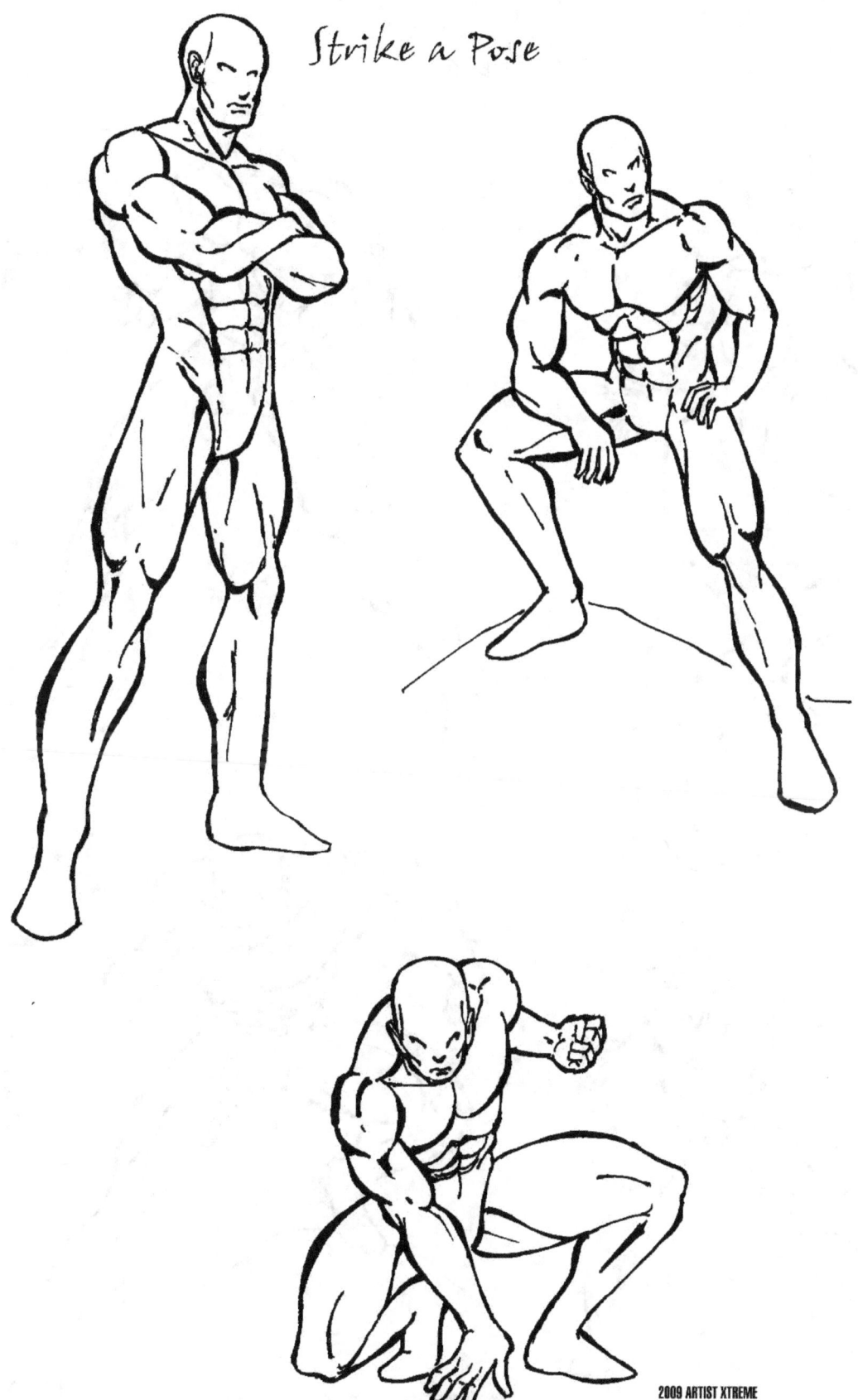

Strike a Pose

2009 ARTIST XTREME

Strike a Pose

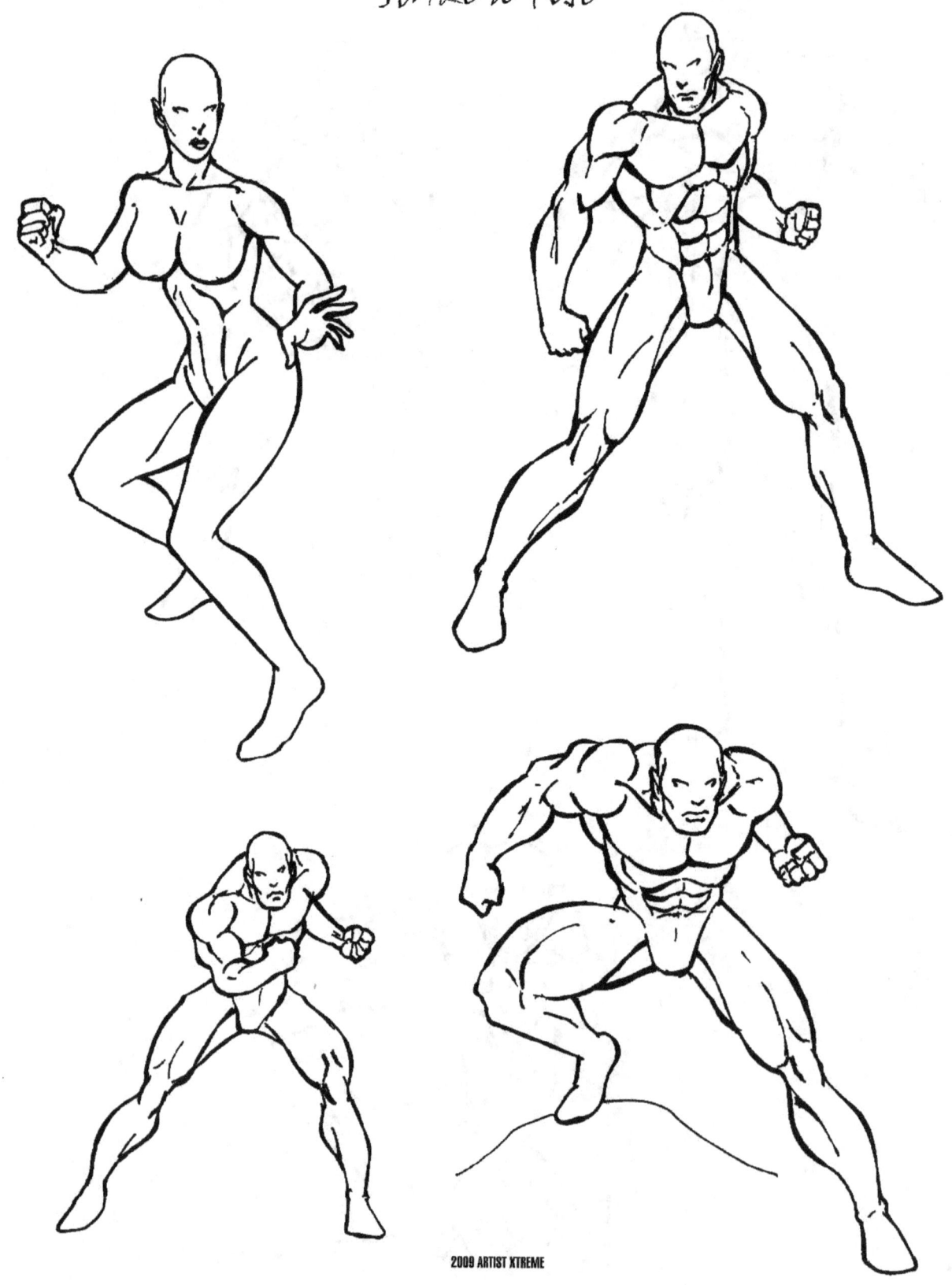

Strike a Pose

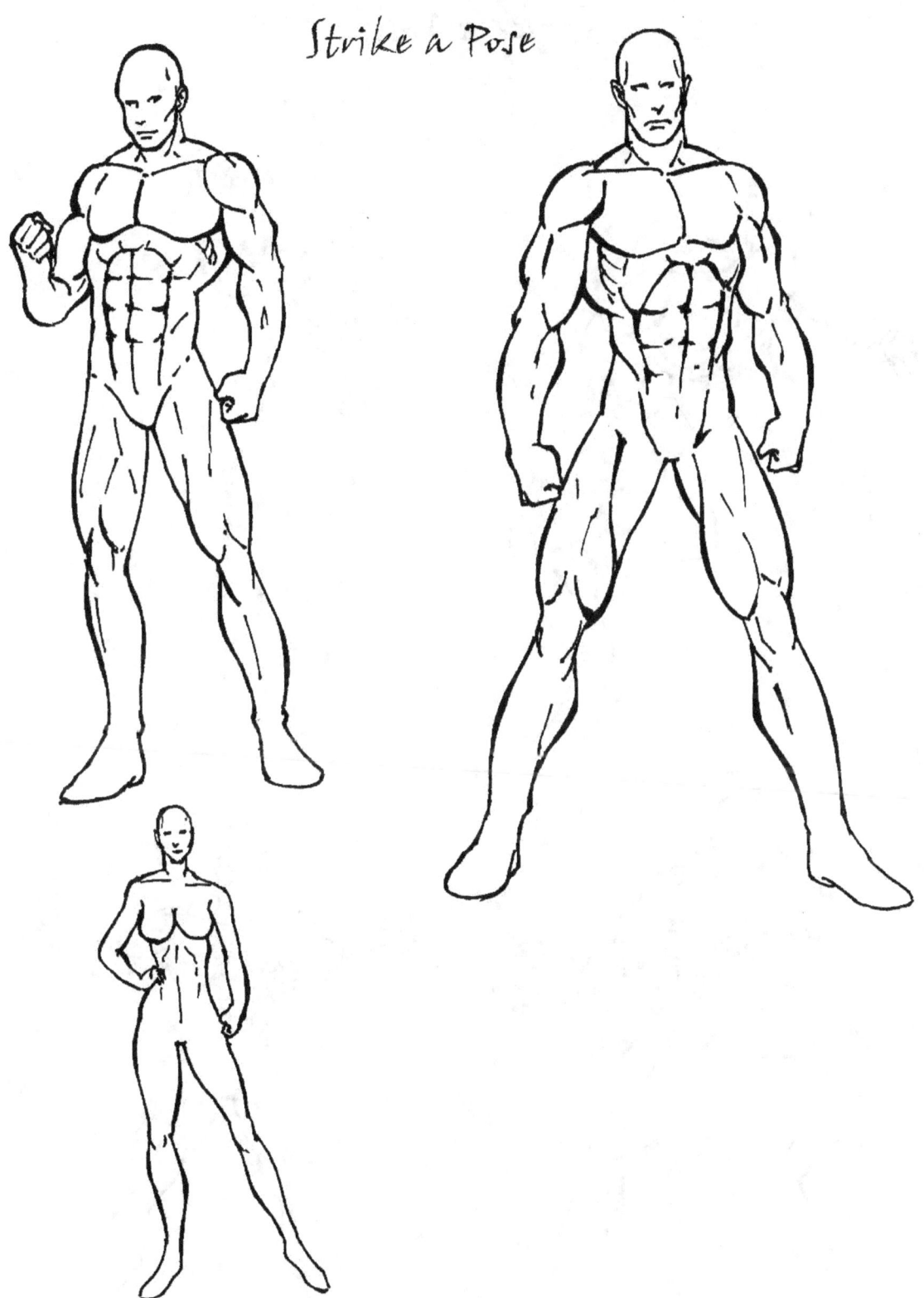

Strike a Pose

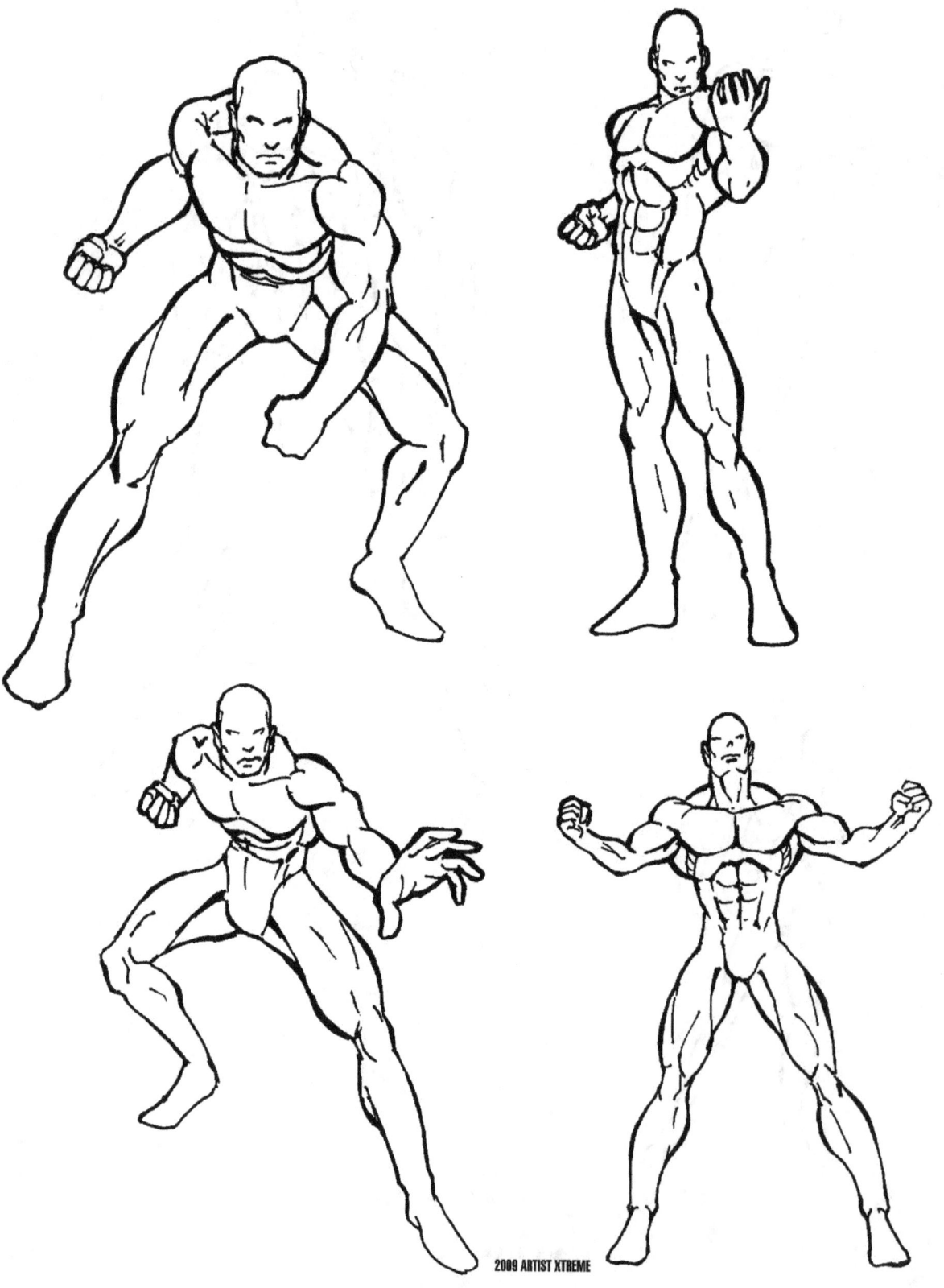

CHAPTER SIX

SWIM

FOR THOSE THAT HAVE A SWIMMING CHARACTER OR JUST WANT TO SHOW SOMEONE SWIMMING,THE POSITIONS ARE SOMEWHAT SIMILAR TO FLYING FOR MORE IDEAS REFER TO THE CAHPTER ON FLYING AND ADJUST THE LEGS TO GIVE A SWIMMING LOOK.

Swim

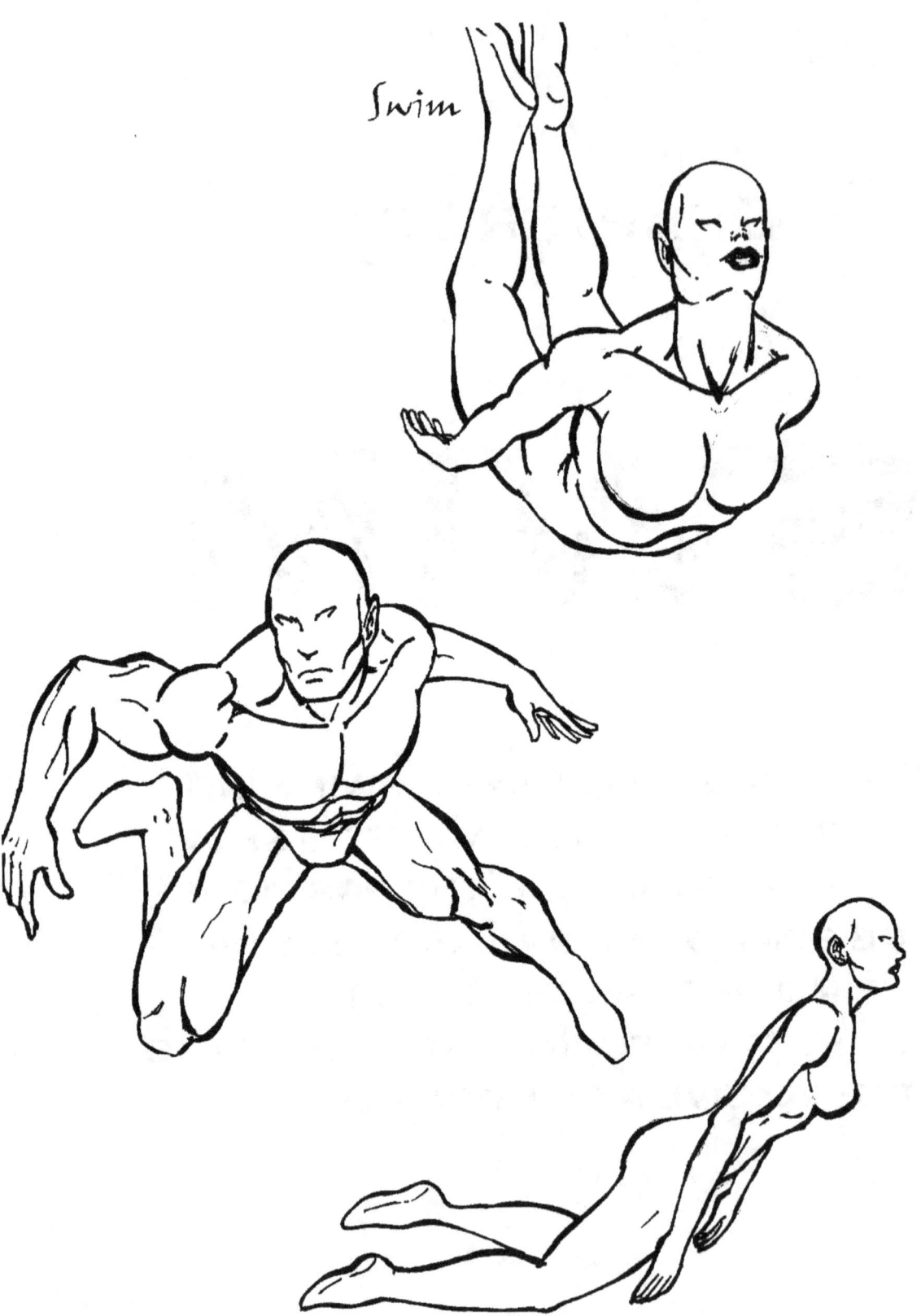

Swim

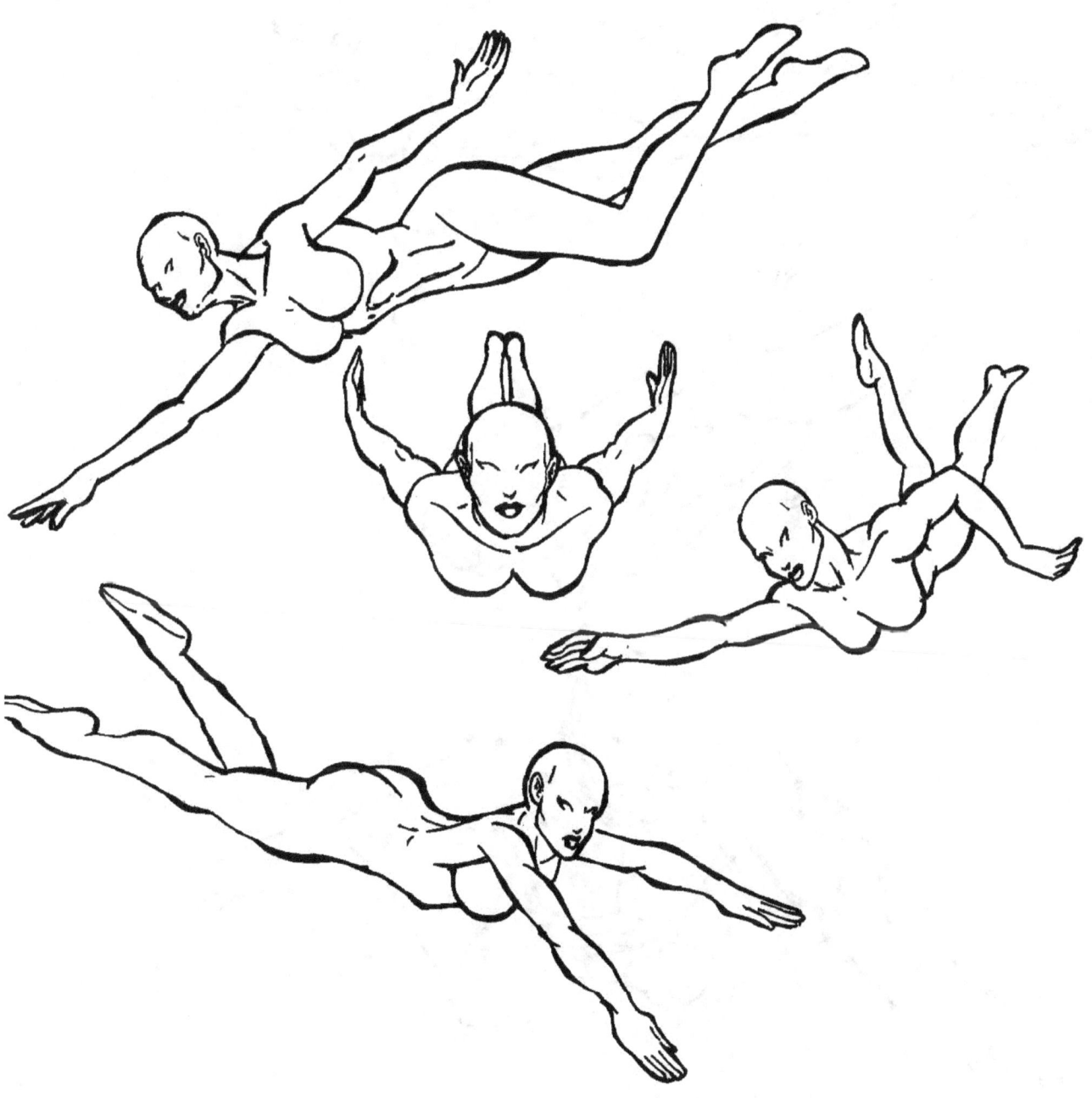

Swim

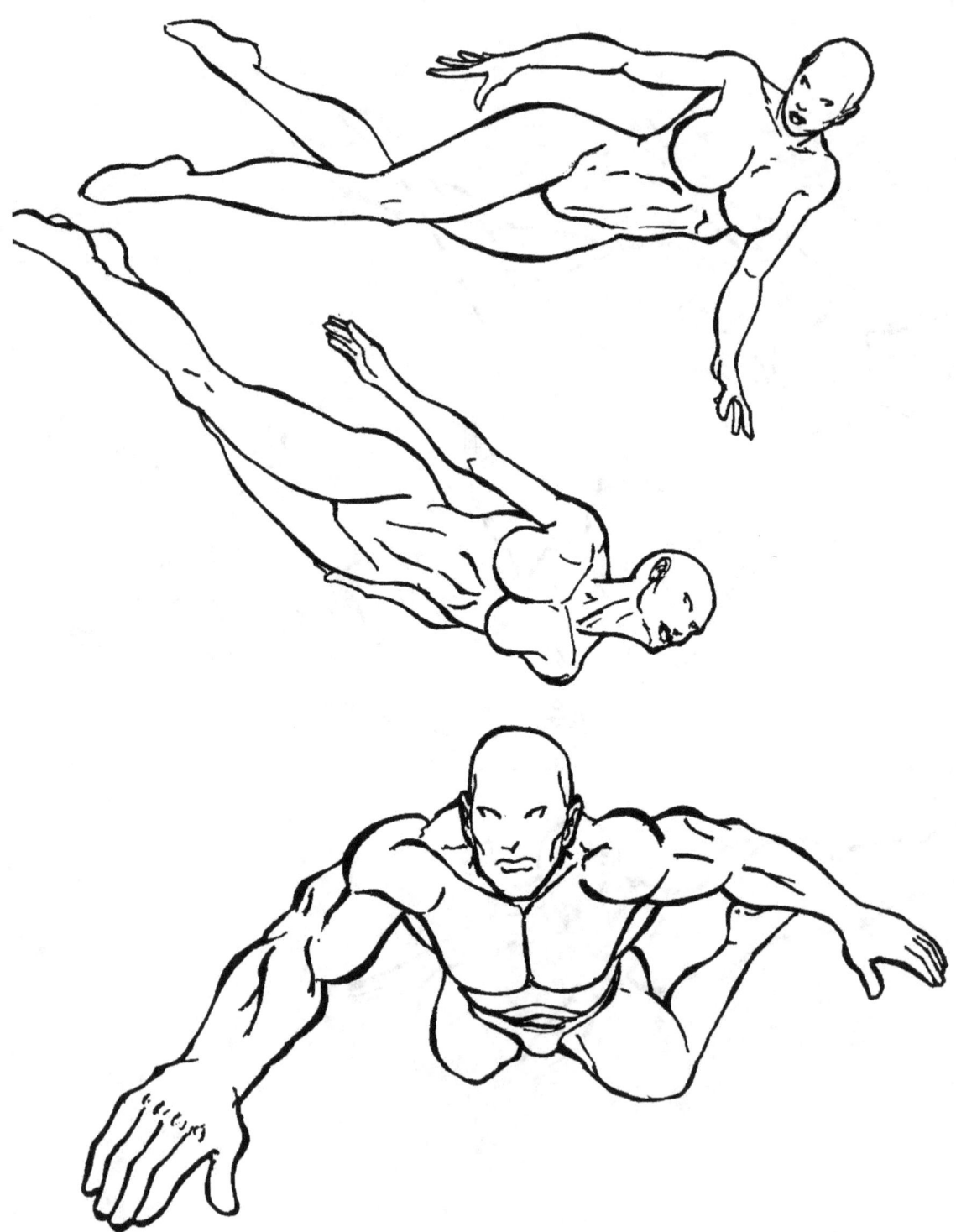

CHAPTER EIGHT

HANDS

IN ANY FIGHT SOMEONE BOUND TO
GRAB A WEAPON, WHETHER IT BE A
ROCK, A CLUB OR AN ATOMIC ATOM
SPLITTER, HERE ARE A FEW HAND
POSITIONS TO HELP YOU OUT.

Hands

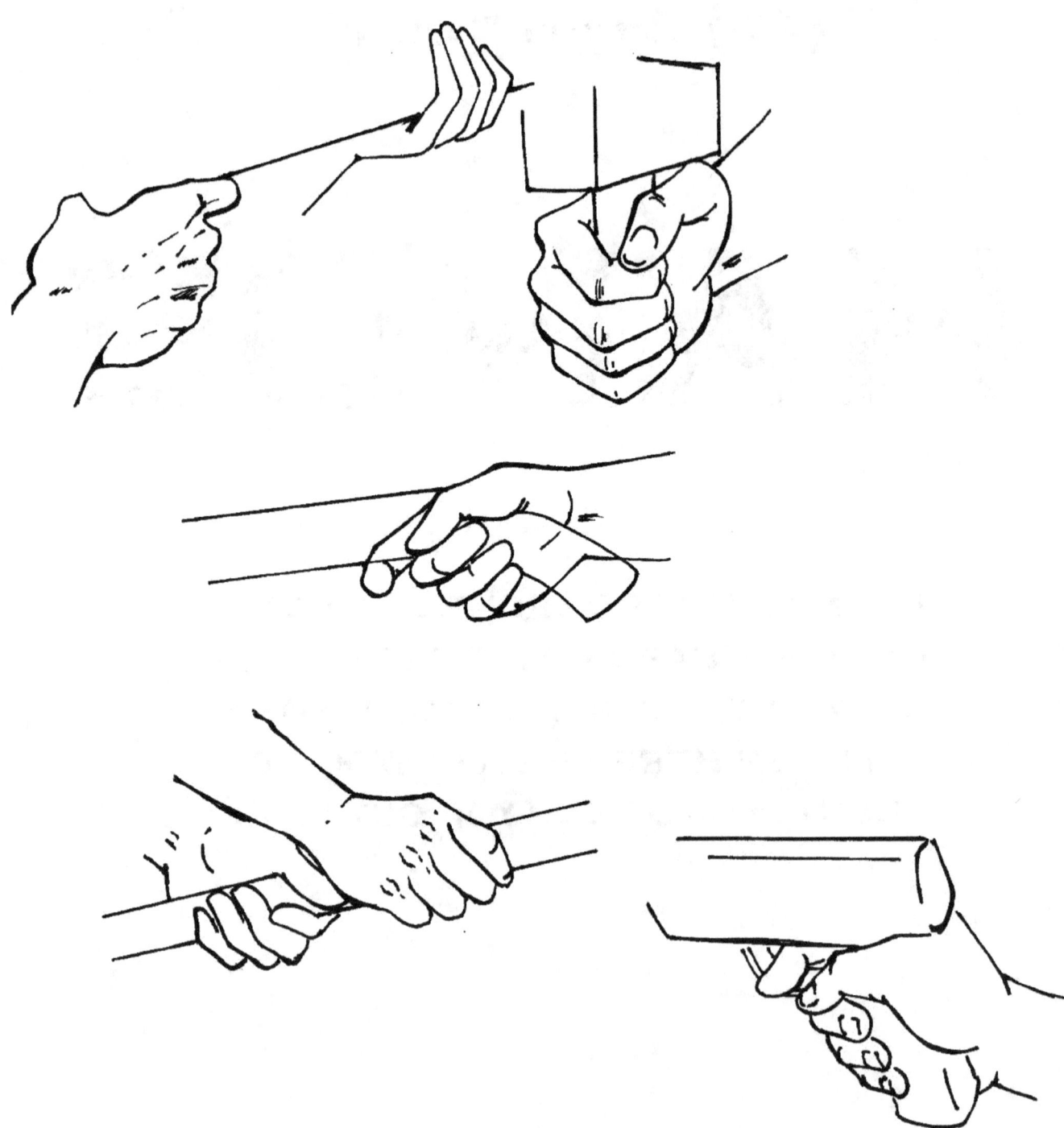

Hands

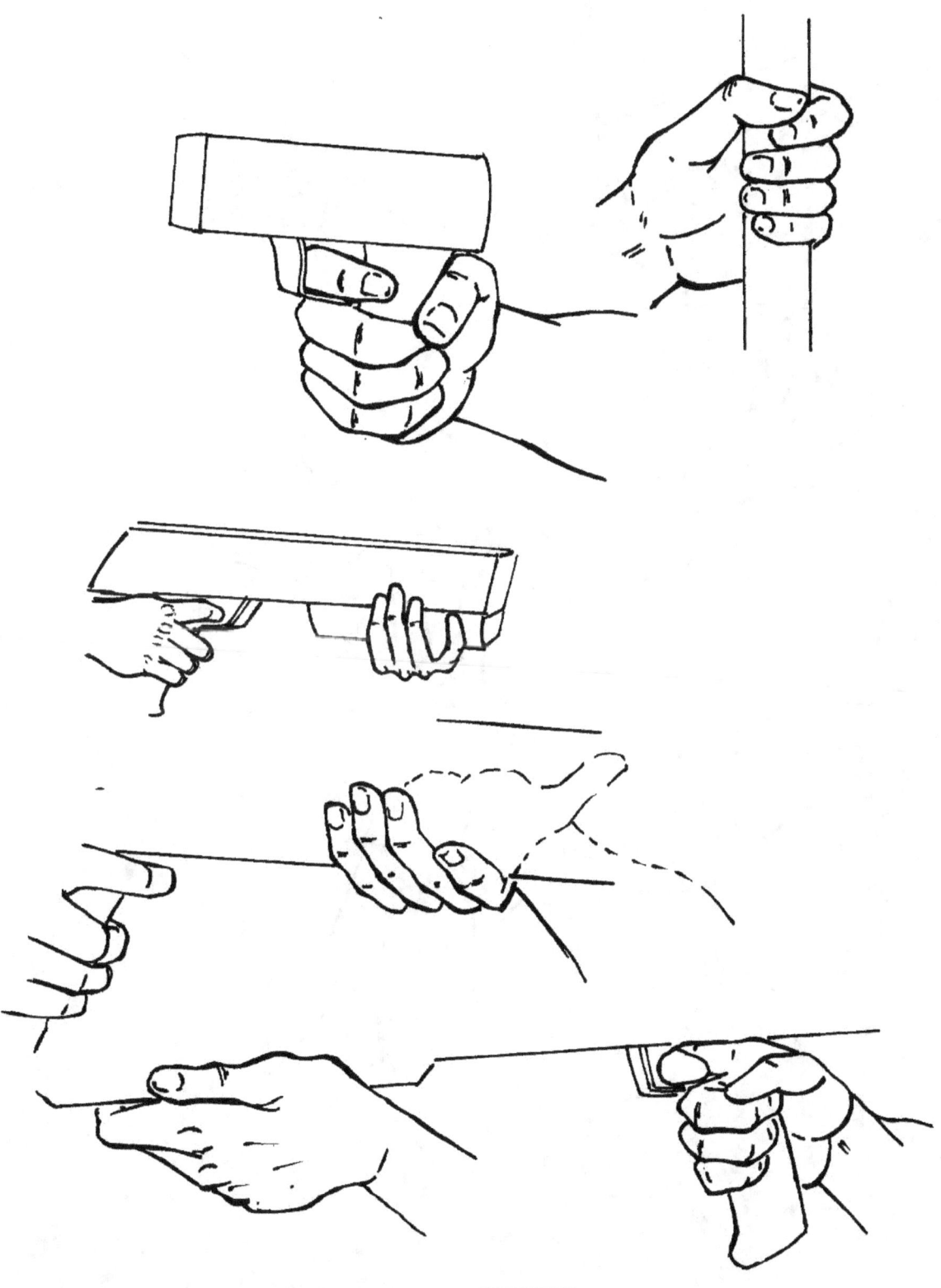

Hands

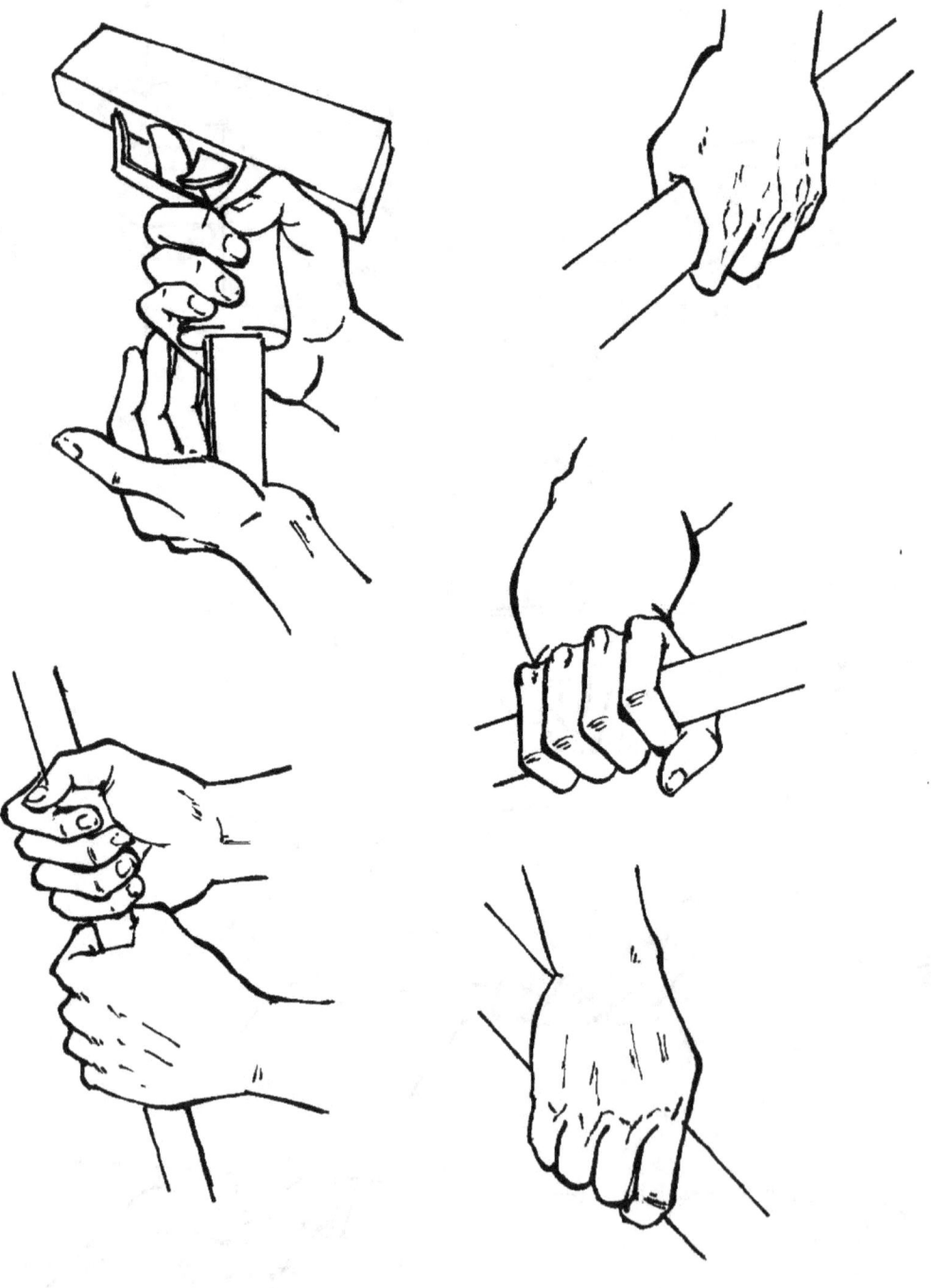

Hands

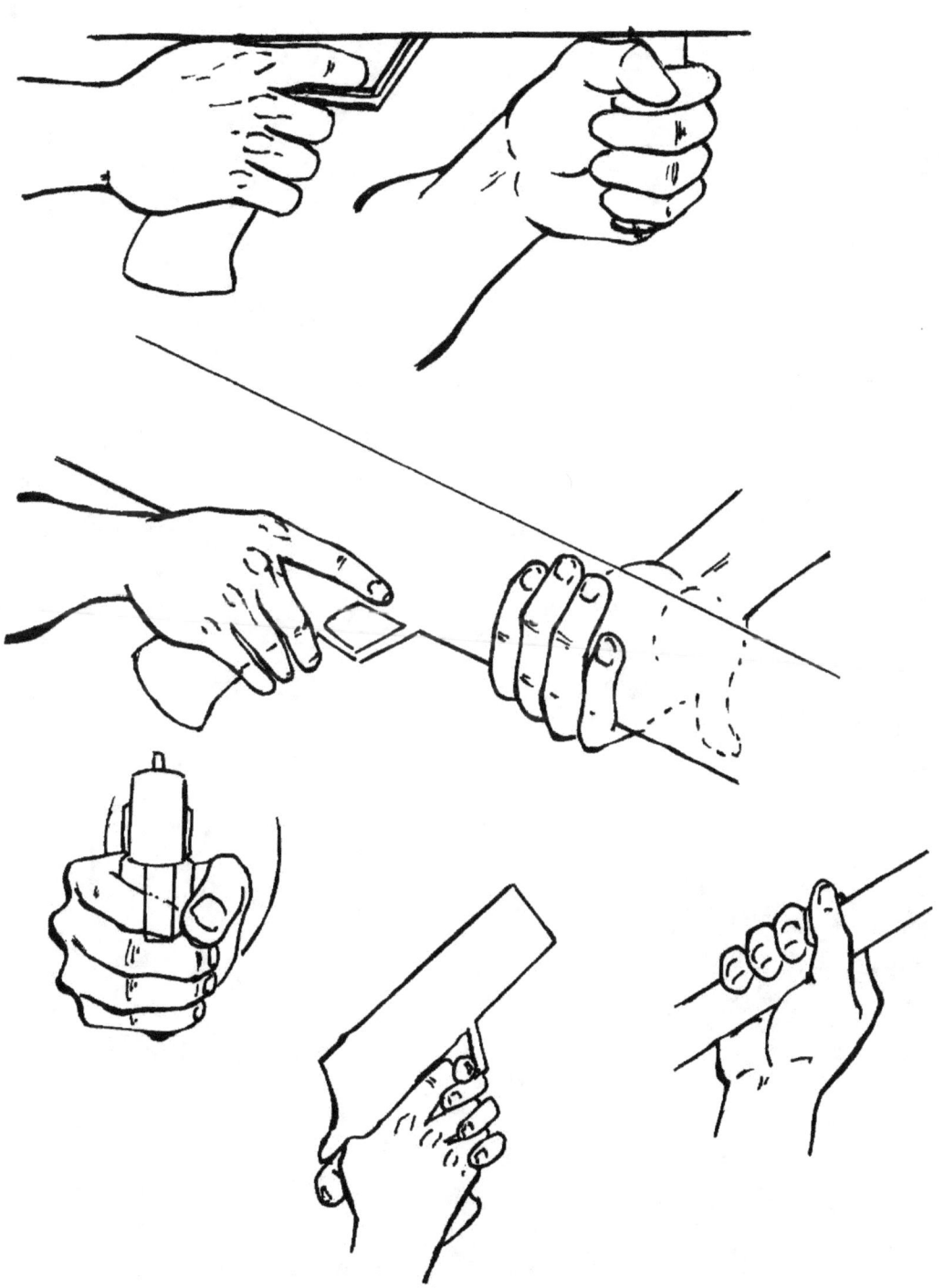